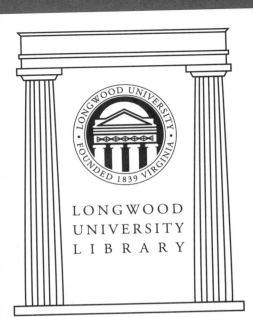

Craft
and
Craftsmen
of the USSR

The found-
ers of art were
potters, black-
smiths and gold-
smiths, men and
women weavers,
stonemasons, carpen-
ters, wood– and stone–
carvers, armorers...
whose delightful artistic
articles fill museums today.

Maxim Gorky

Alexander Milovsky

The Pure Spring

Craft and Craftsmen of the USSR

Translated by Jan Butler
Photographs by the author

**Raduga
Publishers
Moscow**

Translation from the Russian
Designed by *Victor Korolkov*

Александр Миловский

Чистый родник

Рассказы о мастерах народного искусства

Фотографии автора

На английском языке

ISBN 5-05-001181-7

Contents

Russian folk art is often compared to the Firebird, a favourite fairytale character which lights up everything around with its magnificently coloured plumage and makes life beautiful. And the poetic image indeed suits this remarkable phenomenon of folk culture, spiritual and material, which has enhanced people's lives for many centuries. Indeed, it still does so in as far as people nowadays are just as keen on decorating their homes with homespun embroidered towels, carved wooden birds, amusing clay toys and birchbark articles as they are with professional artists' paintings. Interest in folk art and the craftsmen's lives, works and problems is steadily increasing. Books and albums on folk art are quickly sold out; instead of spending their holidays on the Black Sea, students and people of the most varied professions, in no way connected with art eagerly go off to remote old towns and villages to admire the intricate carvings on village houses and meet with the masters still working in the cottage industries' age-old traditions; people looking for gifts for family and friends more often than not head for shops selling folk handicrafts.

Is this nostalgia for a bygone rural way of life or, perhaps, mere conformity to a fashionable craze? Neither, to my mind, but a natural longing, a spiritual need even in this industrial and rational age of ours to commune with that wonderfully naive and magic world which vanished along with childhood.

This is the world of man's infancy when, with tremulous awe and delight, our far-off ancestors followed the good and bad omens of nature, and when the sun, fire on the land and in the sky, storm-clouds and winds gave rise to comprehensible mythological and fairytale images in people's primitive minds. Various peoples, for instance, imagined the sun as a beautiful golden-haired princess, the Firebird, a red horse, a wheel, a golden shield, and the clouds as heavenly herds of animals.

Time out of mind man transferred these poetic images in symbols to the objects all around him such as spinning-wheels, towels, clay toys, crockery, furniture and the walls of houses. The dwelling of an ancient hunter, herdsman or tiller and all his everyday utensils and work tools were essentially miniature copies of his surrounding world. And what we now call folk art was once, and for certain peoples still is a natural and integral facet of life and just like any other ordinary work, such as sowing crops, harvesting or hunting sea-animals.

As the centuries rolled by and mankind advanced, the meaning of these ancient symbols was gradually forgotten by everyone and last of all by the high priests, shamans and magi. Separate parts of this integral picture of the world began slowly to slip away, and then the meaning of others was lost but the coded patterns and designs, displaying amazing vitality and tenacity, withstood the test of time without significant losses, presenting us today with the ancient artists' mysterious and at times still incomprehensible world of ideas.

The world is now changing very rapidly and what until comparatively recently was considered ordinary and universal is now becoming rare and sadly vanishing. For example, a handicraft once in current use in a home is now a decorative piece of art on display in a museum show-case rather than a pantry. This being said, there are still plenty of places in the multinational Soviet Union, in the North or Central Asia, the Baltic republics, the Caucasus, Siberia and the Carpathian Mountains where old folk arts and crafts have kept their secrets and succeeded in competing with much cheaper and more accessible mass-produced goods. And there are still craftsmen working in remote Russian, Caucasian and Central Asian villages whose crafts automatically call to mind the images of the sun's magic spindle and golden spinning-wheel, and beautiful Firebird. Nowadays not only professional artists, art critics and the public at large but also the Soviet Government is devoting considerable attention to the development of folk arts and domestic industries. State resolutions are now being passed with an end to consolidating their material resources, increasing output and improving the quality of articles. Imaginative research is being done into finding new ways of interacting old traditional art forms with modern ones. In a number of republics prestigious honorary titles are awarded to master craftsmen who have won public acclaim.

It is to these folk artists that my book is dedicated.

Inner
Springs

Giving People Sunshine

"A blazing sun offered amicably to a friend on an open palm, a sun resembling a human heart." This is how the poet Eduardas Mieželaitis interpreted the painting *Friendship* which was painted at the beginning of the century by the great Lithuanian artist and musician, Mikaloius Čiurlionis. Celestial fire and terrestrial warmth, the soaring flight of a troubled dream and a poetic perception of the world – was it not for these qualities that Romain Rolland called Čiurlionis the Columbus of a new spiritual continent? In his world of radiant day-dreams, fantasies and universal harmony, all charged with musical rhythms, he sought the revelations of Friendship, Love, Sacrifice, Thought, Truth and Peace. And in his symphonic poems and poetic paintings *Spring Sonata, Žemaičių Kalvarijos* (Zhemaitiyskie Pillars) his source of inspiration in this great quest is invariably folk art and the images and symbols of Lithuanian art.

As a herald bringing us news of beauty, the artist believed that everyone has to be a herald, bearing hope of the past and expectation of the future, and at the end of his way he has to pass his baton on. That is why he admonished those setting out on the road of spiritual quest: "Go on and on without rest, and if your goal is still a very long way off when old age catches up with you, you will see a bench intended for heralds where you will never find a shortage of young people." Čiurlionis proved a prophet.

As a wise Lithuanian saying goes: "Respect the past and the future will respect you!" Lithuanian folk artists constantly bear this in mind, making each new work, aware of the role of their art in returning to the past and linking us with the future.

The Way of Life passes along ordinary earthly roads and it is on these in the first instance that man leaves his mark. In Lithuania with its ritual carved roadside posts (erected to commemorate births and deaths), you understand this like nowhere else. Roads connect people and link time, also, and the genius's creative revelation merely emphasised the wisdom of the original ancient system of symbols.

There are thousands of old roads in Lithuania but the most celebrated and revered – Čiurlionis Road came into being only a few years ago to mark the artist's centenary. Actually, the fifty kilometres of asphalt road between Varena and Druskininkai where Čiurlionis spent his youth and where his museum is now located, existed even earlier but only recently it became known as the Road of Remembrance and the Road of Heralds. It was then that the ancient custom of erecting wooden memorial posts on the hills all along the way was revived. Craftsmen from all over Lithuania came to a summer camp in the small village of Perloj to make the traditional wooden memorial posts. Day and night you could hear the sounds of axes chopping them out of mighty oaks, and of metal jangling in the smithie where Ionas Praninskas was forging "little suns", open-work tops for

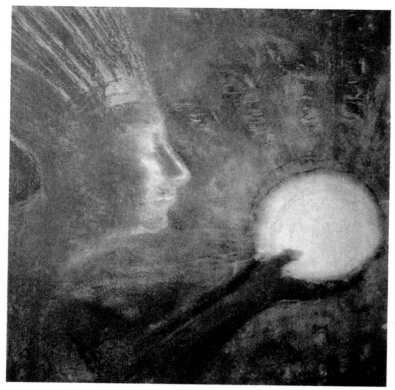

Mikaloius Čiurlionis. Friendship.

them which the artist Čiurlionis was so fond of depicting in his paintings. His memorial road has become a remarkable museum, and its philosophical culmination – the final composition at the entrance to Druskininkai with a bell-post representing Music, a second post, a palette and the third, figures of an old man, a youth and a child, embodying the artist's thoughts on the essence of being so graphically expressed in his admonishment. Its text is carved on a bench under some pines intended for tired heralds bringing news of beauty. And at sunset the blazing sky sets Ionas Praninskas's forged little suns on fire over the sculptures.

Only someone belonging to the Pleiad of Heralds himself could build a road dedicated to creativity, dreams and hopes and, what's more, do so quite self-effacingly, offering people his little suns as gifts. During the war Ionas Praninskas liberated his homeland from the Nazi invaders and then worked for many years as a gardener and agronomist making it more beautiful. And it was only much later when other people of his age were already thinking of retirement after a lifetime of

Metallic "little sun".

work that Ionas, always an artist at heart, suddenly felt drawn towards metal. In his childhood he had sometimes helped the local blacksmith forge horseshoes, axles for carts, and agricultural implements. Over forty years later he realised that he wanted to make iron take on the shapes born of his imagination. He set up a primitive smithy in an old garage and after ten years of hard work he had completely mastered the art of metal forging and could, say, forge the petal of a rose which he had once grown.

13

Fortunately, he became a consummate craftsman just as the Čiurlionis's memorial road was being started, and "little suns" began to arise from his anvil. The main motif of these tops is the sun, often accompanied by the moon, stars and geometrical and vegetable designs and even snakes. The symbol of the sun is undoubtedly connected with old beliefs and rites. As the Lithuanians were the last in Europe to be converted to Christianity – as late as the fourteenth century – the old pagan attributes are extraordinarily vital here. And since the dead are very deeply revered in

Roadside shrine.

Lithuania, the symbol of this reverence became the deified sun with which quite a few legends are bound here.

According to one, the Sun, "God's daughter", is married to the Moon and the stars are their children. When the unfaithful husband started courting the rosy-cheeked Morning-Star Venus, Perkun the Thunder-Bearer seized a sword and smote the Moon's face in half.

According to another, the tsar, the demon of the storm-clouds, enraged by the

14

sun, ordered it to be imprisoned in a specially built tower, and the sun stopped shining. Then the twelve planets, deprived of its light, ordered a huge hammer and struck a hole in the wall with this hammer lightning and freed the sun from its imprisonment inside the icy winter tower. And the mighty blacksmith was none other than Perkun himself, the God of Thunder, who forged people's fates in his smithie among the anvil clouds.

One of the images of Perkun, striking the demons of the clouds with fiery arrows,

Ionas Praninskas. Metallic sculpture at Ablinga.

is a viper, and until quite recently it was strictly forbidden in Lithuania to harm snakes, and killing one was considered a great sin. Sacred grass-snakes were allowed to settle in houses under stoves, and were revered as household gods and offered gifts of milk, cheese, eggs and chickens. And it was regarded as a good sign if they ate the offerings and as an omen of impending disaster if they left them untouched.

It is no wonder that the motif of the sun is highly popular in Lithuanian folk art.

One also finds it in old songs, archeological findings, the patterns on horses' harnesses, the designs of folk ceramics and spinning-wheel distaffs. And just as a sun-shaped cross is a symbol of leave-taking, the forked petals of its cross-pieces, the heavenly bodies, and the sacred groves and grass-snakes are tributes to life, nature and fertility. Thus, Christian and pagan images have been interwoven in a truly marvellous way in this unique form of folk art.

So popular were these delicate metal little suns created by skilled local craftsmen

A "little sun" over the entrance of a café in Vilnius.

that from the 13th to the 19th century they were also used to decorate churches, bell posts, cemetery gates, and tombstones and one would often see trumpeting angels standing peaceably beside coiling snakes. Especially elaborate were the tops of wooden memorial posts, minute models of chapels, which looked just like tiny dolls' houses with wooden figures of gods and saints peeping out of them.

The celestial symbols also used to be present in the burial rites and in the distant past it was customary here to erect tombstones and wooden posts with pictures of the sun, stars, animals and birds. On the Kuršu Spit and in the dunes of the Neringa where the slow-flowing River of Time has failed to wash away ethnographical relics in its way, such posts, made from oak for men and linden-trees for women, are still erected on graves.

The cult of remembrance also signifies faith in the future. Čiurlionis Road is directed towards future generations. It was when he forged his first "little sun" that the spine-chilling word "Ablinga" came into Praninskas's life. Everyone in Lith-

Ionas Praninskas. Posts on Čiurlionis Road.

uania knows the name of this village standing on picturesque hills for all forty-two of its inhabitants were shot dead by the Nazis and the village was razed to the ground at the beginning of the war. And some three decades later sculptors, wood-carvers and blacksmiths came to Ablinga and raised all the executed villagers from ashes, so to speak, by erecting charred black sculptures on the barren hillside. And the ox-eyed daisies now bow their heads to Vladas Baltuonys, Petronéle Srébaliūte, the Žebrauskas and Luožys families and their neighbours. The sculptures arose as if

17

Ionas Praninskas.

Memorial post.

to greet and bid farewell to the day with long shadows, turning them into giants, and to stand guard over and protect the peace for their compatriots. Praninskas's "little suns" over their heads are like halos of mourning and symbols of inextinguishable life.

As the years passed by, the elderly craftsman started thinking about the bench on Heralds' Road. Then he gathered his fellow craftsmen together and told them that he intended to build a good spacious workshop for them all so that the blacksmiths

2*

had a roof over their heads and an anvil of their own to work at. There they would come together to work and teach others and then perhaps one day in the future someone would recall a certain blacksmith by the name of Praninskas. He was given a plot of land in a forest on the outskirts of Vilnius and he and his comrades erected a wonderful turreted wooden house out of their own savings which is now a great tourist attraction. And the hammers of Perkun's grandchildren are now tapping away at liberty and the workshop is gradually becoming a museum of their work. When I visited Ionas, large cardboards were strewn across the floor with designs for chandeliers, wall lamps, candlesticks, door-hinges, lattices and a whole galaxy of "little suns" of all shapes and sizes. Which, I wondered, would Praninskas be forging that day? Perhaps, this one with slender, stiletto-like rays radiating from a large circle and decorated with snakes and intricate open-work patterns which might well be the Knight of the Eternal Sun's coat of arms? Or perhaps the craftsman was not following these sketches but creating something from his imagination at that very moment? I asked him about it as he held a glowing-red finger-width strip of iron over the fire and then removed it with a large pair of black tongs and lowered it onto the anvil, took hold of a hammer about half-way up the handle with his right hand and swung it down over the iron strip. The anvil and other tools around clanged as the blacksmith lifted and lowered his hammer, turning the strip with his left hand, and soon the flattened end of the metal stem took on the shape of a leaf.

"You've guessed right. I don't know what I'm going to make it like yet but I want a lot of light and warmth to come from my 'little sun'. And goodness, too," he added after a moment's thought.

"In that case, Ionas," I replied, "put it up over your front door and let it shine like a beacon for all the heralds bringing tidings of beauty."

The asphalt ribbon of the road cut swiftly through the rocky hillside. Here and there along both sides of the road were piles of large white lime boulders which bulldozers had scooped out of the hillside to make it arable. Then you remembered the parable, which is often told to visitors in Armenia about how God, when he was dividing up the land, gave the Armenians their share last, after all the arable parts had been given out and only bare rocks were left. For, as an Armenian folk saying goes, *Aiastan – karastan* ("Armenia means stone").

"We get our bread from stones," said my companion, Grachya Stepanyan, one of the republic's most famous stonemasons, and he was not exaggerating. Looming in the distance was the sugar-like cone of Mount Ararat, the sentinel of a country of stones. And I recalled the stone-framed blue mirror of Lake Sevan and the black silhouette of the ancient monastery ruins which had stood over the lake for over a thousand years.

Mother Nature mounted the Pearl of Armenia, Lake Sevan, in a stone setting and since the distant past man, imitating nature, has made the stones serve water. To this day in remote and almost inaccessible parts of the Gegard Plateau gigantic boulders known as *vishap*, totems with bull or fish faces carved by people of the Bronze Age thousands of years ago, guard the water springs like priceless gems. Springs here were endowed with miraculous properties long ago for, indeed, what else but a miracle is it to breath life into the stony ground and make wheat and vines grow on it! And the forbidding stone spirits of the springs stand watch eternally.

Some of the springs, which were considered sacred in pagan times, were by tradition revered as such even after the advent of Christianity in 303. This is true, for instance, of the spring in one of the caves of the Gegard Monastery, hewn out of the cliffs which in the 13th century acquired the architectural aspect of a Christian church.

What courage and tremendous faith in man's inexhaustible work potential the anonymous stonemason must have had in order to make the first incision on the cliff top and then start hacking into the basalt, carving huge halls inch by inch out of the hardest rocks.

No doubt he had the same beautiful, slender, sinewy hands, threaded with veins, and the same intelligent, worldly-wise, penetrating eyes as Stepanyan, eyes always reddened from tension and stone dust. Master craftsmen and artists in Armenia are

Sevan Monastery. 9th century.

called *varpets*. The *varpets* who made fountain-heads were revered like saints in ancient times. As I gazed into his deep shining eyes, I could see the pride of a *varpet* who has overcome the fatigue caused by a long life and hard labour.

Stepanyan took me to Echmiadzin where an Armenian stone chronicle bears testimony to seventeen centuries and where many stones have been carved by him. The first spring on the way, one of the thousands in Armenia, issued from a simple stone pedestal near the archway leading to the ruins of Zvartnots, a celebrated seventh-century church. Soon one glimpsed the vast and majestic well-preserved red tufa Church of Ripsime, also seventh century. We had arrived in Echmiadzin.

Along with other stonemasons, Stepanyan has devoted years of hard labour to restoring Armenia's ancient shrines, recalling to mind the distant and quite recent past.

A mere twenty or so steps away from the early-medieval church decorated with the most lavish stone carvings stands a monument carved of grey granite by Stepanyan to commemorate the fiftieth anniversary of the tragic events suffered by the Armenian people in 1915 when large numbers of them were murdered by the Turks.

Vishap—*a forbidding stone spirit of water.*

The monument was made to the design of Stepanyan's great friend, the illustrious and dearly loved Armenian sculptor and architect, Rafael Israelyan. The portal of the Motherland Monument towering above Yerevan was also carved to his design in 1949.

"I liked the design very much," Stepanyan recalled, "I never work if the draft does not appeal to me, but Israelyan had a very subtle feel for the ancient art of carving and continued it, developing the national traditions of small-scale architecture such as small stone pavilions, headstones, fountains, flower troughs, fountain-

23

heads, and marble stelae. It was always a pleasure and joy for me to embody his designs in stone, even when I was working twenty hours a day."

It is impossible for a *varpet* carving other people's designs from stone not to be an artist himself. Most of Stepanyan's works are decorated with his own designs. His creative sources are old Armenian book miniatures, and *khachkars* – cross-shaped carved stones which may be traced back to the memorial and boundary stones of the times of Urartu and pagan Armenia. Be it small or three-metres-high, a *khachkar* is a symbol of a shoot of corn or the sun. It is often so densely decorated

Ruins of Zvartnots. 7th century.

with intricate carvings that its contours of a cross are frequently lost. Whereas originally, over a thousand years ago, the *khachkar* embodied the abstract idea of Christianity and its teachings, with the passing of time, like the most ancient cuneiform stelae, they acquired many other symbolic meanings. After deciphering the inscriptions, it was established that *khachkars* were erected on the most varied occa-

Gegard Monastery. 13th century.
Khachkars *carved in the cliffs.*

25

sions: to commemorate the foundation of a village, the completion of a bridge, the victorious outcome of a battle against an enemy, in gratitude for the bestowal of a plot of land, or as boundary and memorial stones.

While the significance of many may have been lost, as masterpieces of stone-carving and as a unique form of folk art which has given brilliant expression to all the most varied carving techniques and national patterns, thousands of *khachkars*, scattered throughout Armenian towns, monasteries, and churches in the remotest mountainous regions, live on to this day, inspiring a new generation of craftsmen.

Echmiadzin is a unique museum of *khachkars*. Some of the best, oldest stones brought here and placed by the walls of the central alley date from the 9th century, others are marked 1279 and 1543. There is also an 18th-century *khachkar* of the illustrious Pavgos of Goshavank, who has been proclaimed the best sculptor of stone crosses in Armenia's history. A delicate gossamer design appears to have been cast like a cobweb across the white stone's deeply embossed surface. Among the dahlias in the central alley stands an austere and elegant red-tufa *khachkar*. Grachya Stepanyan slows down for this is his work which has been given the honour of standing among the national shrines, one among dozens of the most ancient.

Looking at the filigree relief, I recalled the carved dish, three-millimetres-thick, of grey Gegard felsite which was kept at the Museum of Oriental Art in Moscow, and other of Stepanyan's early works I had been proudly shown at Yerevan's Museum of Armenian Folk Art, and I was happy that the man had eventually turned namely to this craft. You see, Stepanyan became a stonemason quite late in life when he was already a skilled jeweller and metal-chaser.

This change in his artistic life was predetermined by another major event: in 1946, along with many other repatriates he returned home from Iran where his parents had taken him as a child and where they were both buried in Tabriz. It was then that he first started chiselling stone instead of silver and gold as he was used to, and for over thirty years he has never looked back. His stone carvings decorate the Yerevan Station building, the Council of Ministers, the Yerevan market, and houses in Dzhermuk, Dilizhan and Sevan. After making friends with Rafael Israe-lyan, he was drawn towards traditionally national art forms such as *khachkar*, fountain-heads and memorial stones.

Here, in Echmiadzin, the grey or off-white, red and lilac-tinted, black and tobac-co-coloured *khachkars* seem to have entirely captured all the sumptuous beauty of Armenian marble, granite, basalt, tufa and felsite. I asked Stepanyan which stone was his favourite and without waiting for his reply, guessed myself that it had, of course, to be tufa, the most Armenian of all stones.

"Yes, you're right, tufa. Israelyan always wanted me to carve in our very special traditional stone. It's soft but water and wind only make it harder – you've seen that the Echmiadzin church has stood for thirteen hundred years. When I strike a piece of tufa with a chisel, I can always hear an echo. The stone answers me as if it were alive. I've carved my favourite *khachkars* from red tufa. How many of them have I

Grachya Stepanyan.

made?" He could not name the exact figure. "Work it out yourself: on average it takes me two to three months to make a *khachkar*."

Khachkars are Stepanyan's pride and joy, and he has transmitted this love to his fountain-heads, too. The largest in Echmiadzin, which he made in the '50s, is crowned with an eighteenth-century *khachkar* in the traditional manner.

Every fountain-head in Armenia bears an inscription. "Our Lord Jesus Christ, have mercy on Father Mkhitar who has donated one hundred silver pieces to the spring," reads one of the earliest inscriptions, of 1255, on the large fountain-head in

Grachya Stepanyan.
Fountain-head by the Children's Park in Yerevan.

Sevordyatsdzor Gorge on the outskirts of Sanain. "Not anyone may drink this water for my water is special, not anyone may read my script for my script is special," Stepanyan translated the inscription on the white marble memorial fountain-head to the great *ashug*, eighteenth-century poet and composer, Sayat Nova which stands in the very heart of Yerevan. "May there never again be war," reads the inscription on many fountain-heads in Armenian villages, erected in memory of the soldiers who lost their lives in World War II. In Kirovakan you will be shown the house of Megrob, a stonemason who made four fountain-heads in memory of his four sons who were killed defending their country. The row of fountain-heads by the Children's Park in Yerevan are in memory of Alexander Matrosov, Oleg Koshevoy, Alexander Chekalin and ten other heroes of the Great Patriotic War, and, indeed, the memory of these heroes is as fresh as the spring water. A small arch under a gable covering, strictly classical in style, is mounted over these springs.

Water used to be brought to the ancient capital of Armenia, Ani, and to the fortress of Bzhny, through underground clay pipes from a source a long way off – over

Grachya Stepanyan.
Fountain-head in the centre of Yerevan.

ten kilometres away. Reservoirs were carved in the rocks in case of drought or seige, and the springs were very large. For instance, the reservoir of Akhpat Monastery built by Father Superior Ioann in 1258 was thirty square kilometres.

Just as before, a village spring is not just a water source and meeting place where people can find out the latest news, chat to their neighbours and discuss affairs, it is also and, perhaps, first and foremost, a tradition linking different times and generations together. That is why you will never see an iron pipe with a tap here: for this great blessing, water, truly deserves a proper setting.

Fountain-heads have been designed by the master stonemason Grachya Stepanyan in different corners of Armenia. One, for instance, embellishes the gardens opposite Yerevan's Press House. Its façade is decorated with a vine and hanging clusters of grapes, and two stone sheep are kneeling by the water and quenching their thirst. This is the only instance in which Stepanyan has made two copies of the same work: this spring's "double" is to be found in the Italian town of Carrara, Yerevan's twin-town and the home of the famous white marble used by the great sculptors of antiquity. In return, the Italians sent a pair of outstretched marble hands which now stands nearby Stepanyan's spring.

Standing at the crossing of two paths and sheltered from the sun by mighty plane-tree tops, Stepanyan's spring is always cool, even on a hot day. The stonemason and I sat down on a bench in the gardens and watched passers-by stopping at the spring to drink its delicious fresh water. How happy you must feel, Grachya, to know that people will always drink from your springs.

A Deer Speeding Towards the Stars

The beautiful golden-feathered bird soared over the mountains, flapped its wings and the streams, awoken by its warm breath, started tinkling.

The snowdrops were the first to tap their way through their winter shell which has covered the Carpathian Mountains' earth, and to stretch their light-coloured little heads over last year's withered grass. The earth's juices began fermenting, white catkins blossomed on the pussy-willows, and on the southern slope, sheltered from the wind by a beech grove, the dandelions, lungwort, daffodils and gilly-flowers reached up towards the sun...

Bright spring colours are splashed about in whatever direction you care to look from Anna Bobyak's cottage windows. One has to hurry while summer has not managed to dull this brilliant array of colours. But the sudden coming of spring never catches Anna unawares. During the last few days she has gradually selected the largest and whitest eggs from her most prized layers, put bits of black beeswax taken from the hives in autumn into a tin, and assembled her special miniature work tools – the tiny copper-foil funnels with wooden handles she uses for painting eggs.

Anna, one of the best artists of Kosmach, has got everything ready at home to transfer all the hues of spring to her eggs. This custom is countless centuries old.

> *Out of the egg, from the lower part,*
> *Came raw Mother Earth;*
> *Out of the egg, from the upper part,*
> *Soared the high vault of the sky;*
> *Out of the yolk,*
> *The shining sun rose up;*
> *Out of the white,*
> *The clear moon did shine...*

This marvellous egg, the cradle of the Universe, was laid by a duck in whose guise, according to the Finnish epic *Kalevala*, the Almighty God Unko himself appeared to the maiden of the sky and mother of water, Ilmatar-Kava. The idea of the Universe emerging from an egg first appeared in ancient Indo-Iranian legends. According to a legend recorded by Herodotus, the world was hatched from an egg which had been placed in Helios's sanctuary by the mythical Phoenix bird. Several Greek and Roman philosophers also mention that the Universe originated from an egg, and the idea then came to Old Slavonic manuscripts from Byzantian sources.

The spherical sky makes up the top half of the shell, and the subterranean world, the lower half.

In the opinion of the eminent historian and Russian folklore collector, Alexander Afanasiev, cosmogonical myths are, in fact, tales about the renewal of nature in spring. In mythology, the egg, as a metaphor of the sun and lightning, is seen as a symbol of nature's renaissance in spring, and as the source of its creative force. When cold winter breathes death and destruction over the earth and sky, the embryo of future life is concealed in this egg, and with the coming of spring, a new

Anna Bobyak. Hand-painted eggs.

world is created from it. Then there is the ancient poetic notion of the rising sun being born of the night's dark depths, and the spring sun of the thunder-clouds, and of the sun's golden egg being laid by the black bird of the night or bird of the anvil cloud. In such myths a cockerel often personified both dawn and lightning to an equal degree.

In many peoples' legends and tales the golden eggs are laid by a hen or duck. In one Russian tale, for instance, a man shut a little duck up in a dark shed and during the night she laid a golden egg. And when the man came into the shed and saw a

Anna Bobyak.

great blazing light, he reckoned the shed had caught fire, and shouted out at the top of his voice, "Fire! Fire! Missus, grab a bucket and fetch some water!" But when they opened the shed, they saw neither flames nor smoke but only a dazzling golden egg...

The speckled hen's golden egg is found not only in folktales. In folk art, for instance, the painted Easter eggs – *pisanki* – from the picturesque archaic region of the Huzul Carpathians where every spring the beautiful old folk custom flourishes again, give us some idea of our remote ancestors' views of life. The delicate art of painting eggs is passed down from mother to daughter, generation after generation. Anna Bobyak was taught by her mother, and one day her own daughters' turn will come too.

Painting eggs is a ritual, and, what's more, a festive ritual and that's why in the early morning Anna went into her living-room, beautifully decorated with brightly-coloured hand-towels and embroidered curtains, opened the family trunk standing by the wall, containing family heirlooms such as bead-embroidered caftans, a wonderful 19th-century Huzul hatchet with a copper chased pattern and even an old pistol with an octahedral barrel, and took out a white embroidered blouse and a skirt suitable for a special occasion. And dressed in her festive national costume, Anna looked even more beautiful.

Then she sat down at a small table and set a dish of eggs in front of her, and her husband, Dmitry, brought in a cast-iron pot full of glowing coals to keep the tin of wax hot while she worked. There were five or six little foil cones filled with hot molten wax in the tin.

Anna picked up an egg with her left hand and the cone's wooden handle with her right, and ran the cone lightly across her palm, leaving a light dark-brown smear of cold wax. After a moment's thought, she confidently drew a straight line all the way round the egg, and leaving a gap, another one parallel to it. Next she drew diamonds, triangles, and spirals on the top half of the egg, and on the very tip the outlines of two deer set among stars, a popular design in the village of Kosmach.

Then Anna picked up another egg and drew wavy lines across it. The amazingly imaginative Huzul artists who are keeping this old art form alive create so many different pictures and patterns on the egg's small surface that among a thousand it is practically impossible to find two alike.

The technique of painting eggs is very distinctive and somewhat similar to that of printing coloured designs on textiles – *batik*.* First, the contours of the pattern are traced with molten wax and they keep their original white seen when the egg is dipped into a little pot of yellow paint. After the first coat of paint is applied, the cone's fine tip is again run smoothly over the egg's surface, leaving a line of molten wax. The egg is then soaked in a pot of orange paint and a yellow pattern is left under the second series of wax lines. And this process is repeated over and over again

---

* In *batik* the design is drawn with a thin layer of wax and then the material is dipped in paint which dyes the parts of the cloth untouched by wax.– *Auth.*

with the patterns being traced, and then the egg being dipped in darker reds, burgundies, browns and blacks.

Anna held a jet-black egg over the coals and wiped the swollen wax off it with a soft cloth and the egg started glittering with dozens of rainbows! And at last you could see all the intricate details of the artist's design, the perfect geometrical pattern and harmonious colour scheme. No wonder Kosmach painted eggs are considered the most beautiful.

The egg is then smeared with lard or covered with a thin layer of transparent lacquer to make the pattern glossy and the colours fast. In time the yolk will dry up and shrink into a hard lump and start rattling inside the shell and the white will turn to dust but the egg's painted surface will keep perfect for decades, enabling future generations to admire all the splendour of these Ukrainian miniature paintings. In museums a tiny hole is sometimes made in the shell with a needle, the contents extracted with a syringe and the egg filled with wax to make the valuable exhibit less fragile. Some collections boast eggs over a hundred years old whose colours are still just as bright as ever. Whereas artist nowadays use aniline dyes, in the old days they used natural ones specially prepared from tree bark, horsetail and other plants.

"It takes from fifteen minutes to several hours to paint one egg, depending on how complicated the design is," Anna told me, and there certainly are a great many different ones.

All these designs, both complex and simple, and even the individual lines and strokes once had a definite symbolic or magic meaning. According to traditional folk beliefs, the painted egg itself was a symbol of the spring, the sun, the regeneration of nature and life. Hence, the great popularity of the "tree of life" motif in the guise of twigs, flowers, fluffy bushes, leaves, little fir trees and ears of corn. The painted ear of corn also symbolizes a bumper harvest, calling to mind the fact that the Ukraine has been a major granary of Europe for a very long time indeed.

As symbols of prosperity, the Carpathian Mountains animals are also lavishly depicted on the painted eggs in the form of stylized ponies, deer, sheep, goats, doves, cockerels, hens, cuckoos, moths, crayfish and fish.

But what if we were not only to decipher separate symbols of the painted egg but also to regard its wonderful mosaic pattern as a complex integral composition reflecting the ancient idea of the egg as a microcosm of the world? In that case, its diamond-shaped "equator" symbolizes the Earth, the spherical surface above – the skies, and the spiral pattern – the course of the rising and setting sun. But then how did the branch-antled deer come to be among the stars on the top of the world?

Neither local legends nor Slav folklore have provided a direct answer to this question. But, you see, the art of the Carpathian Mountains region has retained echoes of a cattle-breeding and even hunting mode of life in which deer-hunting was an important livelihood. The answer should possibly be sought in archeological and ethnographical data on the peoples for whom hunting still forms a major integral part of their daily lives unlike the Ukrainians who have been farming the land since time

35

immemorial. After the most fascinating research Academician Boris Rybakov came up with a brilliant solution to this problem. He succeeded in finding the key to the mystery of the celestial deer in the myths of the Ugrian-Samodiitsy primitive hunting tribes, and pictures on the bronze Ugrian-Perm shamans' pendants and in a shaman's grave in a Mesolithic cemetery of the some seven thousand years old at Oleny (Deer) Island on Onezhskoye Lake. It appeared that Anna Bobyak and the other Huzul artists from Kosmach who depicted deer in a starry sky on their Easter eggs were conveying to us the idea of primitive Mesolithic hunters seven thousand years ago about the two celestial deer rulers of the world. So that is how far in time the thread of memory may be stretched thanks to artistic images in folk art.

And the painted eggs of today also give one insight into man's world outlook in all the interim eras as well. For instance, whereas a netting pattern betokens a good catch of fish, the fish is no longer a symbol of ancient pagan beliefs but an attribute of Christianity which took their place. The new religion also "cribbed" the octagonal star, once a symbol of the Sun God, now that of Christ. And the eggs themselves were linked to the celebration of Easter. The dots once depicting stars in the sky now also represent the tears Mary shed before implacable Pontius Pilate. The triangle became a sign of the Holy Trinity. The continuous different-patterned bands round the egg symbolize eternity. Signs of spring's renaissance on the painted eggs became symbols of human goodness and concord. In spring people give the painted eggs to their dearest and nearest as tokens of affection and friendship and girls give their best eggs to their boyfriends, sometimes as symbols of their consent to marriage. Eggs with pictures of a hen and cockerel are given to childless married women. And the cockerel on a painted egg is a sign of prosperity and wellbeing. Elderly Huzul villagers who have quarrelled exchange eggs as symbols of reconciliation. Gaily painted eggs were hung across the walls of a room alternately with bunches of corncobs, not only as decorations but also to protect the house from thunder and lightning. And when paper wings and tails and a wax head were added to them, they turned into brightly-coloured little doves hovering below the ceiling.

Over the centuries a great many tales and legends have sprung up around the painted eggs. According to a particularly lovely old Huzul legend, if the custom of painting eggs is ever forgotten, a chained monster will break free and destroy life on our planet. In years when only a few eggs are painted, the monster's fetters loosen, and great disasters befall the earth. And when many are painted, the monster is chained fast and love triumphs over evil.

...Anna Bobyak's work was drawing to an end. She wiped the wax off the last eggs with a cloth. Some of the painted eggs are slightly less bright than others.

Anna Bobyak. Hand-painted egg. Fragment.

"These are shop eggs," she explained. "Their shells are too smooth and even and not so porous and the paint doesn't stick to them as well."

The pile of eggs was growing, reminding us that the folk art of painted eggs was continuing to flourish in Kosmach, where, indeed, it had reached its zenith. The infertile rocky soil here was unsuitable for cultivation and so crafts arose instead; painting eggs became a profession for women who then sold their wares at spring fairs. Tomorrow morning Anna and Dmitry would go round the village giving away their painted eggs to neighbours as gifts and getting others in return. And their daughter, smiling confusedly, would ask to be left the most beautiful one. And one could certainly envy whoever was fortunate enough to receive her gift.

It was a good spring that year. In many houses bees wax was being melted and the simple tools got ready just like in the old days. The monster was chained fast, and no evil would befall Kosmach.

No Pogo, No Wedding

May there always be firewood before your hearth,
And babes in cradles besides,
May children toddle before you,
And livestock behind.
May your life be long,
And your health be strong till your hair turn grey.

These words were half-spoken, half-chanted to the newly-weds by the match-maker, swaying her body in time. The wedding ceremony which, according to ancient customs, lasts several days in Khakasia* was in full swing and I was still gaping in wonder, no, not at the bride, though she was very pretty indeed but at the elderly wrinkled match-maker, Taira Abdina from the village of Sapogovo. You see, I had never been to a wedding before where the match-maker was more beauti-fully dressed than the bride. And it was the *pogo* that did it – the beautiful enigmatic *pogo* – which, according to tradition, only the match-maker could wear and only for the duration of the wedding. The other special feature of the ceremony was that the match-maker could not be unmarried or childless.

The *pogo*, the main but not the only obligatory part of the ritual dress, was worn over an embroidered waistcoat which, depending on the time of the year, was worn over a smock or fur coat. The match-maker also had to wear a fur hat and long shoulder-length silver earrings with large corals. And these earrings were so big and heavy that they were fastened to the head with wire and braid.

The embroidery in Khakasia is bright and colourful, and the *pogo*, a bib embroi-dered all over with beads, corals and mother-of-pearl, is the decorative costume's crowning glory. Though of an infinite variety, *pogo* are highly formalistic in shape, size and decorative style. They also contain very many symbols: in shape they resemble a bud with two curved upward-pointing petals. The central pattern is either heart-shaped or conventionally designed. It is formed by the large mother-of-pearl circles or buttons easily recognizable as the eyes, nose and ears of an anthro-pomorphic mask which may sometimes have a third eye on its forehead. The *pogo*'s patterns consist of close rows of spirally twisted thread, beads, shiny gold and silver sequins, always edged with a row of mother-of-pearl buttons and fringed with

---

* Khakas Autonomous Region is in south-eastern Siberia.– *Ed.*

bugles.* A genuine *pogo* was always a costly garment. It used to be given as a dowry, and years were spent saving up to buy the corals, semi-precious stones and mother-of-pearl for its decoration.

The *pogo*'s pattern resembles a human face so much because it traditionally depicts Mother Umai, the ancient goddess of fertility, continuer of the family and guardian of children's souls. Shaman used to set off to her dwelling beyond the clouds with incantations to ask her to send children to childless families.

The *pogo* on Taira Abdina's front was ablaze with light vying with the sun. She

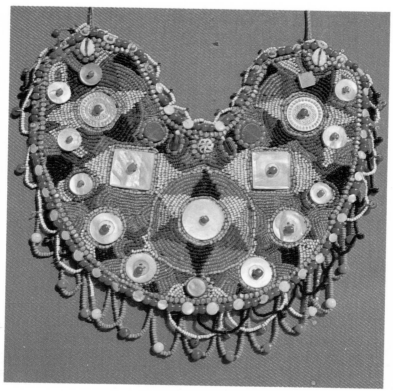

Old pogo.

embroidered this *pogo* herself. "It's long and hard work making a *pogo*," she had told me the day before. "First you have to cut out several strips of material in the shape of a bib. Then they all have to be soaked in glue. And when the bib has dried, the thick and supple cloth is ready to be embroidered." The *pogo* is embroidered without a preliminary drawing. The needlewoman designs the pattern herself and keeps it in her head. First of all, large mother-of-pearl circles are sewn in a strictly symmetrical pattern and then finer stitches are added, and the spaces between them

* bugles – tube-shaped glass or plastic beads.– *Tr.*

40

Taira Abdina.

filled with beads. The bugles are sewn on last. The material used for the embroidered pattern is so bright and colourful that tremendous artistic taste is required of the needlewoman for if the colour scheme goes wrong, the article may turn out crude and gaudy.

But now let us go back to the wedding ceremony. The match-maker leads the young couple out of the traditional summer yurt which has been made specially for them, and starts walking round it, bowing towards the east where the sun rises. Behind, holding onto her hem, comes the bride, bowing like the match-maker who

Taira Abdina. Pogo.

by tradition performs the role of her mother during the wedding ceremony, for the bride's parents do not participate in the ritual. Then the young couple go inside the yurt and bow down to the fire, thereby taking the vow of marital fidelity.

Now it is time to untie the bride's plaits – *syurmes* – and plait two stiff braids known as *tulun* which married women are accustomed to wear. Hence the name of the wedding day – *sas toi*, the festival of hair. By tradition, a shin of mutton from the wedding feast is wrapped in a white cloth and tossed among the bridegroom's young men friends. And each tries to catch it as it is considered that the one who

42

gets it, will soon be happily married himself.

So far everything has taken place on the bridegroom's "home territory" but now messengers are sent to the bride's parents to set the day for the newly-weds' arrival. While the bridegroom's friends compete in contests of strength and dexterity, Taira Abdina tells me about the *pogo* which she has embroidered for her own two daughters and daughter-in-law one day. Every household has to have a *pogo* for sooner or later the time will come when it is needed and the Goddess of Fertility will look at the match-maker from the *pogo* and bless yet another conjugal union and

become the good companion and guardian of yet another happy Khakas family.

This custom goes back so far in time that its meaning has been erased from human memory long ago. Perhaps, the *pogo*'s secret is kept in the Khakas steppe by the no less enigmatic idols, popularly known as *inei tas* – stone grannies. You see, on many of these statues, which are about six thousand years old, the stonemason also chiselled a *pogo*! These statues, which are ten times older than those on the Easter Island, and much more lavish in design and symbols, are also linked here with the Goddess of Fertility. And perhaps there is indeed a direct link between the *pogo* of so long ago and the one seen at Khakas weddings today? This secret may, however, always be kept by the Goddess Umai's impenetrable face.

According to a Yakut legend, the horse was the first living creature in the world, from which first the half-horse-half-man and then eventually man originated. The Yakuts used to worship a deity called *Dyesegei*, who was supposedly the creator and patron of horses and appeared in the guise of this animal. The *Ysyakh* festival whose origin is linked with the Yakut people's forefather, Ellei, is also closely linked to the cult of the horse.

"Far, far away to the north you will find a beautiful country where people breed cattle. There your descendents will multiply." So Ellei was told by his dying father who had been unable to endure all the sufferings of the long and hard journey. Ellei carried out his father's last wish and led his people to the middle course of the Siberian River Lena where the Yakuts, a Turkic-language people of horse-breeders, still live to this day. And many centuries ago their distant ancestors really did come to the north-east of the Asiatic continent from the Lake Baikal area, the Altai Mountains and the steppes of Central Asia, leaving vestiges of their enigmatic past in the mysterious cliff signs and rocks drawings along the River Lena's banks, in the heroic folk epic *Olonkho*, and in legends, songs, dances and rituals, and bringing with them the cult of the horse which is the main animal they breed among Lena's lakes and forests, just as it once was long, long ago in the boundless southern plains.

Horses used to be offered as sacrifices to the chief god, the creator of the Universe, *Yurung ainy toion*, who, it was believed in antiquity, inhabited a wonderful country in the ninth heaven where there was no winter and where there was grass as white as the wings of a swan. It is, therefore, understandable why both the horse-breeders' festival of *Ysyakh* during which shaman sprinkled fires with fermented mare's milk, and the ritual mare's milk bowls (*chorons*) used for this ceremony were particularly revered by the Yakut people. Of all the Yakut people's utensils the carved wooden *chorons* were the most beautiful. At the *Ysyakh* festival the man making the appeal (*algis*) to god would stand in front of the fire, holding the largest bowl of mare's milk in his hands and after finishing the first part of the appeal in which he had colourfully described in detail all the preparations in the deities' honour, he would sprinkle the fire three times with mare's milk and then make petitions to the deities.

When the ceremony was over, the festival's organisers would settle the assembled company on the grass in separate groups comprising elderly and honoured guests,

poor people, and women and children, and offer the mare's milk to them all. The first large *choron* would be brought to the most revered guests and then they would pass it on to the person on their left side and so on round in a circle. Often the repast consisted of nothing else but sometimes well-off hosts offered their guests meat and buttered porridge known as *salamat* as well.

When the repast was over, national games were played, singers entertained, and storytellers performed the heroic Yakut epic *Olonkho* amidst cries of approval from the audience. Late in the evening or during the night if the weather was fine, horse-back races were organised and the whole festival passed in a noisy and lively atmosphere.

...After flying about seven thousand kilometres from Moscow, here I was in the old Yakut village of Suntar in the upper reaches of the Siberian River Vilyui. In this region once famed for its *Ysyakh* festivals, supposedly the very best in the whole of Yakutia, ancient traditions and folk art are preserved with great care. Indeed, the ancient festival lives on, as do its legends, rituals, songs and dances. And so, too, does the art of making *chorons* and other carved wooden vessels.

Nowadays at the festival boys and girls dressed in national costumes perform a dance in which they hold a small *choron* and mime the ritual pouring of mare's

Choron. *19th century.*

milk. I already knew that these *chorons* were made by Grigory Savvin, an architect of the Suntar district, and one of Yakutia's best craftsmen, who spent all his free time carving wood. His works are on exhibit at the Museum of Folk Art of the Russian Federation in Moscow and at the Museum of Ethnography of the Peoples of the USSR in Leningrad. I visited him at home and found him busy at work. As it was a hot day, he had settled down with a whole array of chisels and knives on the ground outside his studio door.

In Yakutia these traditional ritual wooden vessels are either large and tall with tapering stems or broad and short with three stems shaped like horses' hooves. It is said that when the legendary figure Ellei was riding across the river to his new homeland, he looked in the water and suddenly saw the horses' stables, foals' stalls and various kinds of vessels for mare's milk which he later made after this manner.

The vessels' austere and economical decorative pattern consists of usually three, seven or nine horizontal bands around the top as these are sacred numbers for the Yakut people, and here signify the degree of respect or reverence felt for the people the *choron* was intended for. The oldest and most honoured guest at the *Ysyakh* fes-

tival was always offered a vessel with nine bands for as we have already mentioned, according to a legend, the creator of the Universe, *Yurung ainy toion* lived in the ninth heaven.

Time out of mind only skilled craftsmen attempted to make these vessels for the Yakuts reckoned a mediocre craftsman's hands would start aching and withering if he were to try. Looking at Savvin's works, which are elegant in form, exquisite in design and superb in quality one finds no cause for concern about his health. Indeed, they may be compared to any of the best old vessels of their kind.

"Well, you could say, I started making these vessels quite by chance," the craftsman told me. "About fifteen years ago I had to go into hospital and to kill time I started carving wood and got so interested in it that I've kept at it ever since. I was fascinated by these wooden vessels and the better I got to know them, the more I admired our old craftsmen who succeeded in making with the most primitive tools such extraordinary smooth, and perfectly proportioned vessels that the Yakut *choron* may withstand comparison with antique vases. What's more, each of them is unique not only in design but also in proportions, which give it such harmony. And whereas in its traditional carved patterns you can see something similar to those of other Turkic peoples, in form the Yakut *chorons* are quite unique. If you were to

At the Ysyakh *festival.*

look into its origin, you would discover that some *chorons* are shaped like a Scythian cauldron, once again reaffirming the links between these ancient cultures. The low *chorons* on three stems in the form of horses' hooves were supposed to transmit to the person drinking fermented mare's milk from it the power of the horse, a sacred animal. The tall slender *chorons* on one stem are like the silhouette of a dancing crane. Following the white crane northward, a favourite and revered bird among the Yakut people, their ancestors once came to this beautiful fertile land, for, after all, where else could the homeland of this majestic bird be?"

Grigory Savvin.

As I listened to Grigory and learnt the secrets of the *choron*'s beauty, unusual durability and capacity for lasting not just decades but even hundreds of years, I could not help marvelling over and over again at the ancient craftsmen's profound and astute understanding of the laws of harmony and beauty and of the qualities of the wood – supple, tough and quickly drying birch, which I already knew well from Arkhangelsk crafts. Before they started carving these wooden bowls, it appeared that these craftsmen first boiled the wood in milk to make it softer and then let it dry out. They used the most primitive tools – an axe and a sharp round scraper and a knife with a curved tip for carving the vessel inside. And they used to carve the pattern with an ordinary knife with a sharp narrow blade. The Yakut craftsmen's consummate skill was appraised by Academician A. Middendorf, one of the top experts on Siberia, thus: "The tremendous versatile manner in which the Yakut succeeds in using the blade of his knife enables him to substitute it for a great many different tools. When he wants, for instance, to make a bowl, he will at once bend his knife in a bow against a tree trunk and before you know it, will be carving a bowl out of wood... There's always something remarkably stylish about whatever he carves."

The finished *choron* was never painted or varnished but boiled in cream or oil which soaked into the vessel and made it tougher and more resistent to moisture and gave it a dark mellow colour.

"The wooden bowls' circular pattern," continued Grigory Savvin, "is based on the principle of continuity and eternity, and the way it is carved depends on what it is intended for: if it is for everyday use, it has a shallow carving and for festive occasions it has to be deeply carved, and the most honoured ritual vessels with nine bands are decorated with three-dimensional relief carving. The craftsman has full discretion to choose from a wide range of patterns, including loops, diamonds, arches, triangles, silhouettes, netting and hearts. Each of them symbolizes the horse, cow, deer and other animals. Time-hallowed art and wisdom – this is what makes the wooden bowls beautiful."

The master paused for a while, lost in thought and then picked up his three-edged chisel again and gently touched the pale supple piece of wood out of which he was going to make a large wooden bowl with nine bands for the next *Ysyakh* festival in Suntar.

...Meanwhile the festival was in full swing in a green glade bordered with birch trees. The children who were very beautifully performing the national dance, were holding small *chorons* with three bands as they, of course, were not old enough to hold such a splendid bowl. And they were drinking the frothy mare's milk, a favourite delicacy of mortals and gods, with obvious relish.

The Home Hearth

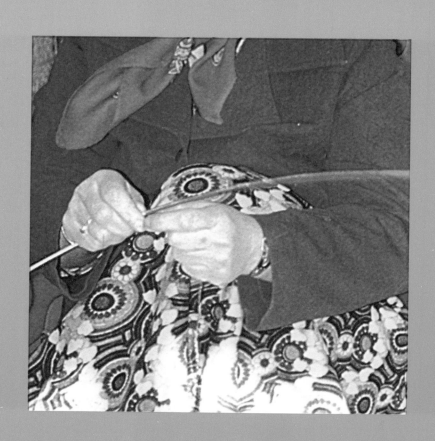

The beautiful yurt was standing not in a pasture's luscious green grass but on a museum's slippery parquet floor, and it was illuminated not by the rays of the mountain sun but by the chilly light of a cut-glass chandelier. Its exotic appearance in this contemporary setting aroused mixed feelings among the museum's visitors: curiosity among the tourists, admiration among the artists and bitter-sweet memories for a grey-haired old Kirghizian villager.

Time reaps changes, and even in mountainous Kirghizia, people are now building brick and mud houses. Today there are hardly any yurts left in Kirghizia except for in the summer mountain pastures and for this purpose the most primitive dark-brown felt yurts are quite adequate. Nevertheless, over the centuries this nomadic dwelling has acquired the ideal structure of a portable home and the comfortable, elegant, austere and beautifully decorated interior for which it is now famous.

The yurt is not only a masterpiece of Kirghizian constructive design but also a superb work of art for all the most prolific Kirghizian folk art forms have been applied to its decoration. Indeed, everything in it is lavishly decorated, from the latticed walls made of a series of curved planks, the painted poles supporting the dome and the carved wooden doors to the household utensils, such as stamped leather vessels for mare's milk and *chyi*, cane mats.

So, have this masterpiece of folk design and all the numerous crafts linked to it really become mere museum curios? No, I was assured in the Kiyal Folk Industries Association, which was founded in 1968, uniting craftsmen from the remotest corners of the republic, the Kirghizian yurt is still thriving, and so are the wonderful traditions of mountainous Kirghizia's folk art.

> *The sheep were sheared...*
> *The girls started rolling the fleece,*
> *They teaseled the fluff,*
> *They spun the yarn,*
> *They made the felt.*

These lines from the Kirghizian epic *Manas* describe how felt was made for the legendary Manas and his warriors. The complex labour-consuming work remained unchanged for centuries and it took many days of hard work to turn the fleece into felt, a hard-wearing fabric used for many objects of everyday use and works of folk art, such as yurts, bags for storing vessels, and carpets. Kirghizian rugs are said to

Dzhumamedinn Sukayev's team erecting a yurt.

be as spacious as steppes and as bright as a mountain meadow when the tulips are in bloom.

There are two types of felt rugs – *ala kiyiz* and *shyrdak*. The coloured pattern of the first type is rolled into the single-coloured fabric while the felt is being made and in the process the pattern loses its distinct outlines and becomes soft and diffuse.

The *shyrdak* is brighter, and its coloured pattern, concise and symmetrical. This type of rug is perhaps more common than the *ala kiyiz*. Nowadays it is made by the

appliqué method: two layers of different-coloured felt are laid out and the pattern is designed on the top layer and then the "layered cake" is cut into pieces along the pattern's lines and the pieces are all sown together again in such a way that the ornament comes from the top layer and the background from the lower one. The seams are disguised with coloured cord and to make it more durable and warmer, the rug is quilted with one more layer of felt. A classic example of a bicoloured *shyrdak* is a rug whose pattern on one side is a mirror reflection of the one on the other side, the only difference being that the ornament and background exchange colours. However, the multicoloured *shyrdaks* are the most beautiful. Such a rug demands expert precision, virtuosity and a developed colour sense. The rugs are not

55

made to a conventional pattern; each time the craftswoman creates a new combination of colours and patterns.

There is no longer any need for the craftswomen to make the felt themselves as it is manufactured at factories and, what's more, from a very wide range of colours. And the Kiyal Association has given a new lease of life to the old craft of rug-making, one of the most fascinating forms of Kirghizian folk art. Asil Ibraimova from the Chkalov Collective Farm in the Talass Valley in the west of the republic is one of Kiyal's best rug-makers. All the floors of her spacious house are covered with

Asil Ibraimova and her daughter, Nuripa.

wonderful multicoloured *shyrdaks*. And just now she and her daughter Nuripa, who has come home from her institute for the holidays, are finishing a large decorative rug. All they have left to do is sew coloured cord along its edges and it will be completely ready. Asil is working nimbly with a thick needle. Looking at this attractive youthful woman, it is hard to believe that she is the mother of eleven. Asil

Asil Ibraimova. Shyrdak. *Fragment.*

learnt the art of rug-making from her mother who, in turn, learnt it from Asil's grandmother.

"I really love making rugs," she tells me, "I love creating new patterns which reflect old motifs. For example, *kaikalak* – ram's horn – a looped or spiral pattern, or *karga tyrmak* – crow's claws – a kind of shamrock pattern. Unfortunately, the names and even the meaning of many old patterns have been lost. In the old days they helped you to discover the author's intention and his ideas of life. They reflected his dreams of having fertile flocks of sheep and fast horses with flowing manes, the smoky atmosphere of nomadic camps and the whistle of hunting arrows. My grandmother still remembered some of this. I'm very glad there's a new demand for my handiwork. True, the old craftswomen are dying out and the young are still at schools and institutes and leaving home like my children. But I believe that my little Giulsara who's now in the second form will one day take up my craft."

A few houses away in the next street lives Giulshair Alibayeva, a celebrated weaver, who makes patterned runners on her hand loom to cover walls, floors, yurts and beds. Giulshair is seated in a far corner of the room and woollen threads, taut as strings all colours of the rainbow, are pouring out from under her hands in a fan. Her hands are moving so fast, it is at first hard to follow what she is doing and you only remember the last movement in complicated process when she adds yet another layer of threads to the tough thick fabric strip with its austere geometrical ornament known as *taitaka*. Then you gradually begin to see the various other motions of the shuttle, the tool for lifting the top layer of thread and needle along which the ornament is woven.

We won't disturb her as she has to memorize the whole complex sequence of the shuttle's movements to keep the pattern's precise lines. We'll move on instead to the village of Aral, and the home of Ruzbai Anishev, one of the few saddlers left in Kirghizia.

The valley narrows on the way to Aral and the road is hemmed in by sea-buckthorn bushes, out of which frightened pheasants keep springing onto the road. At last, the bushes come to an end and only mountains stretch on ahead as far as the eye can see. Hundreds of horses are walking down from the upper pastures, one after the other, in a chain, a kilometre long. The herdsman's beautiful bay is striding out slightly to one side. The horseman in a tall astrakhan hat passes by slowly with a fixed expression on his deeply wrinkled face. Perhaps he was thinking of his herd for his hand was playing with the whip.

And what a whip it was too! Even from a distance you could see that this thin taut switch of very fine leather lashes had been made by skilled hands. The tarnished inlaid silver pattern on the saddle gleamed dimly.

"That's Ruzbai's work for sure," my companion, Turusbek Alimbekov, a Kiyal team-leader, informed me.

...Bridles, whips, cruppers, girths, breast-collars, stirrups, pendants and brushes were hanging all along the fence, and spread across a table and floor planks in Ruzbai Anishev's yard. The most beautiful among all these intricate articles was a new saddle of glossy leather and metal, shining like silver. Armed with a little hammer and a range of chisels and punches, the saddler was making a design of diamonds, spirals, crosses and stars on its shiny metal discs, large breast-plate and stirrups.

I asked him about the whip we had just seen. "Yes", he replied, "I made it. I plait them out of eight strips but my father used to make even more beautiful ones like snake scales out of only two strips. I have no idea how he did it because I never

Old yurt's interior.

managed to learn his secret."

He picked up eight narrow yellow leather lashes from the table, pressed them between two fingers at the top, started tying the first knot.

There are over a thousand craftsmen in the Kiyal Association and each of them is helping to develop the ancient crafts of this people who were nomads until quite recently.

...Nurganesh Asanova lives in Frunze in an apartment furnished just like any other with a dresser, table, sofa and chairs. On a wall, however, hangs a magnificent rug with an exquisite traditional pattern, the like of which you might see in a museum.

"Yes, this is a *chyi*," Nurganesh told me with a smile. "It means grass or cane in Kirghizian. It grows in the steppe and is picked in September. Its stalks are thick like straw and it is up to one and a half metres high. Once the stalk has been cleaned and the dry leaves stripped off, you can make anything you like from the smooth, even and stiff stalk: an *ashkana chyi*, matting between the kitchen and the store rooms, an *eshik chyi* – hanging doors, a *chigdan*, a matting in which a yurt is rolled, and bags and boxes.

"My parents were shepherds and we lived in a yurt in Issyk-Kul where, it just so happened, the biggest cane grew. My mother knew how to make lots of things from them and I used to help her and that's how I learnt all the details of this craft. But nowadays hardly anyone remembers this curious craft although it's needed by people. I'm quite sure articles made of these canes would look very attractive in modern town apartments too."

She sat down at the table, picked up a bunch of golden canes, laid them in a neat row, close to one another, and then weaved the edges together with thread into a mat. But this was only the beginning – the hardest part still lay ahead. With light pin pricks Nurganesh marked out the future pattern on each cane. I could not guess what it would be like from the faint dots but I realised it already existed not only on the mat in her hands but also in her mind's eye.

Now the mat was split up into individual canes again and woollen or silk thread was wrapped round and round each one on the parts marked by the pin pricks so that the canes joined together to form a pattern. When all the canes had been woven together, Nurganesh used a wooden press to flatten them. Cane mats come in all sizes. It takes about two weeks to make a medium-sized mat and this small one would be ready much sooner. These reeds are commonly used in the handicrafts of many Oriental peoples, so let's hope cane articles will brighten up the homes of many Kirghiz generations to come.

If the white hills had not changed shape and drifted away in a different order, I would have taken them for white mountain peaks, especially as there really were mountains beyond the ravine by Issyk-Kul. As the crow flew, the lake was only about eight kilometres away.

It was a clear cold morning. The strong wind from the mountains chased pillars of dust ahead and there was no chance of putting up the yurt. But Dzhumamedinn had warned me about the wind the evening before and told me it would die down by eleven. So I waited impatiently to see if the team-leader's predictions would come true. And, sure enough, by half-past ten the wind did abate, only to gather strength for an evening attack on the mountains. Such was the way of nature in these parts: the wind changing as regularly as tides, blows from Tien Shan in the morning and from the lake in the evening. Ak-Terek stands half-way along this huge air corridor.

It was namely here, near Issyk-Kul, that a team of twelve skilled yurt-makers, consisting mainly of women, worked under the supervision of Dzhumamedinn Sukayev. I was told that the finished segments were assembled in one of the large house's rooms and then put together and tested out in the yard outside. I knew that all the parts of a yurt had just been finished in the house but that it was only going to be assembled in a week's time when the customers from the Kiyal Coop brought a vehicle to collect it.

After drinking about five bowls of green tea that evening, the team-leader gave in to my requests and agreed to talk the other team-members into erecting the yurt

Ruzbai Anishev.

before the customers arrived. Now, it was not quick work erecting a yurt.

Once the wind had died down, Dzhumamedinn and I set off to fetch the carpenter, Toktosun Ismailov, who lived on the other bank of the fast-flowing river which tumbled noisily over the rocks towards Issyk-Kul. We found him at work in his yard, standing by a bench and bending the tips of some long wooden poles, over three metres long. The ends of the poles were sticking out of a pile of sheep dung and chopped straw. "The poles have to steam there for about two weeks until they bend easily and keep the shape I'll give them on the bench," the carpenter explained.

61

"Then after they've been in a clamp for a few days, they're ready for painting."

Leaning against the wall of the house was a large stack of finished bright red poles – the framework of the yurt's roof. We slung them over our shoulders and headed back to Sukayev's house where we found the whole team already waiting for us.

What would soon be an elegant yurt was for the time being a pile of packages, planks and poles, and a roll of thick felt which entirely filled the room. We dragged it all outside and put it down near the platform on which the yurt was going to be erected. With natural ease the women unwound the braid with which the *kerege*, lattice walls, would be fastened together, and started to stretch them out at intervals in a circle, about six metres in circumference. Once stretched out, the red wooden lattices became slightly convex. The women then tied them together with straps, and soon the shoulder-high wall was ready and only an opening for the door had still to be made. *Tizgich*, handwoven braid, secured them along the top of the lattices.

Now came a key point in the work: the roof was to be erected. Holding onto the lower ends of the poles, the women slotted their tips into special holes in a huge wooden hoop. Then Dzhumamedinn lifted this entire construction on top of the walls with a pole and his assistants quickly tied the bottoms of the poles to the top of the walls. At last, the hoop was erected (its hole would serve as a flue) and the construction, firmly secured.

The next stage was to line the inside of the lattice wall with a long strip of cane matting called *chigdan* which would protect the yurt from wind and dust, without preventing ventilation. The team had this done in a few minutes because all they had to do was unroll the tightly wrapped rolls of matting and press them up against the lattice walls. Then they fitted the painted door in place.

Next came the most laborious part of the work – covering the roof with the very heavy felt and only Dzhumamedinn could manage this. After hooking the edge of the felt cover with a long pole, he lifted it over his head and only on a third attempt succeeded in tossing its edge over the hoop. His helpers quickly caught the rope dangling from the cover on the opposite side and pulling all together, dragged the thick white felt over the frame, and now half the spherical roof was ready. The operation was repeated step by step, and the second half of the roof was soon in place, too. The felt was then secured and several ropes slung over it and tightly fastened, and now no wind would be of danger to the erected dwelling.

But just then there was no sign of any wind for it had hidden in the mountains from the midday heat. Down below the ravine was shrouded in a mist and Issyk-Kul had vanished.

Casa Maré

Translated literally from the Moldavian, "*casa maré*" means "a large house" or even "a great house", although it is not a house at all but just one room and not even lived in. What's more, it is not even a sitting room but a very special room where the family gathers together only on festive occasions. It has, however, been an essential part of every Moldavian village home since the times of Ancient Rome, many of whose cultural traditions the Moldavian people have in common.

But even if the Moldavians had not inherited from the Romans this tradition of keeping such a room, they would still have been forced to invent one for it is namely here in this room that they are able to give full expression to their remarkable and quite unique predilection for interior design. And it's not just a predilection but a natural flare for introducing into a room's overall composition a vast number of the most varied everyday objects, ranging from embroidered cushions to smart festive dresses.

And notwithstanding all the diversity and improvisation in a *casa maré* it is not hard to notice certain general rules which are abided by. For instance, the centre of the main room is left empty and on ordinary days occupied by a large loom which the mistress of the house works at, and all the furniture and decorations are set along the walls. This is where all the very best articles in the house are traditionally kept and the things which other people might store in a large wrought-iron trunk are hung along the walls here: beautiful embroidered towels with lace edges, a carpet, and usually more than one, and neat piles of hand-woven carpet runners, floor-cloths, canvases and rugs are laid on narrow benches along the walls. If there is a sofa or bed in the room, it is always covered with lots of embroidered cushions. Hanging in a corner are shawls and head scarfs, folded in four. Sometimes the walls themselves are painted in a bright and florid manner. Often in a *casa maré* you will also find photographs of family members in patterned frames, and bowls of fruit, biscuits and sweets. Every flat surface is covered with several layers of mats, striped rugs and towels. In some houses there are still wonderful antique wooden beds, benches with chiselled backs, open dressers for crockery and painted trunks.

The walls, ceilings, skirting-boards, window-frames and platbands are all decorated in a *casa maré* for every Moldavian is an artist at heart and the *casa maré* is his canvas. If there is not enough material for decorating the room, the mistress of the house will always find something – even a piece of sheepskin to pin over a bare spot. All these seemingly fortuitous things, thanks to her impeccable artistic taste, make up a unique harmonious composition known as a *casa maré*.

"The most important decoration in a *casa maré* is a large wall carpet, 'rezboi', which means 'war'," Nadezhda Roshka, one of the best craftswomen of the village of Khiliutsa in North Moldavia told me. She then went on to explain that when a carpet of this kind was woven on an almost vertical wooden frame, each warp thread was pulled through with such force that it looked as if the weaver was battling with the material.

The wall carpet in Nadezhda Roshka's *casa maré*, covering the entire surface, had an unusual pattern of large dark-red dahlias on a black background and light-coloured sheafs of corn. The symbolism was very clear – tireless work on the land and the celebration of beauty which the land gives people, and people then transfer to the *casa maré*.

"I was given this carpet as part of my dowry by my mother," said Nadezhda, "mind you, the sheafs of corn weren't on it then – I added them myself when I grew up. And this rug here on the sofa I made thirteen years ago when I had my daughter Raya – it's the first item of her dowry. Almost everything in this room – the rugs, cushions and runners will be hers one day too. And this wedding handtowel I made for my daughter too, and its special day will come too. I tried to make it even more beautiful than the one my mother once made for me. You see, in our part of the world wedding towels are only used during the wedding celebrations and by them you can tell how highly regarded and closely related the people are seated at the wedding feast, for the brighter and more decorative the cloth, the closer the guest is to their hosts.

"And this carpet runner called a *kandrena* and sometimes a *makatul*, I remember especially well because it was the first piece of work I did all by myself on a loom. That's how it is here: when you live with your parents, you help your mother and only do all the work yourself when you move into your husband's house."

Moldavian carpet-making is an old craft. In the mid-17th century a historian by the name of Paul of Aleppo stayed in Moldavia on his way across Russia with his father, Makarius, Patriarch of Antioch, and mentioned the craft in his account of the journey. These smooth carpets are woven like a tapestry. They used to be made in nearly every home and the craft gradually became a tradition: a bride had to have carpets as part of her dowry as symbols of her hard work and skill.

They are still woven on wooden looms at home and the masterly weavers also weave cloths with ornaments which look like the most intricate embroidery.

"The warp threads are from spools bought in a shop but the weft ones are from home-dyed wool," explained Nadezhda.

Moldavian carpet-makers try to achieve a contrasting effect. For instance, the motifs of the patterns in the middle and along the edges are always different, and the colour combinations of the designs and background contrast.

As for the designs themselves, they have undergone noticeable changes over the years. Whereas the favourite pattern in the 18th-century carpets, which have been

Nadezhda Roshka.

preserved, consists of exquisite slender outstretching stems of plants whose lines break off sharply, and concise geometrical designs, from the 19th century onwards the central part of the carpet comprised more realistic flowers and bouquets. Variations on the floral theme still predominate in homewoven Moldavian carpets today. However, there are no set rules as far as its colour scheme goes, and it may be as varied as the weaver sees fit.

The Moldavians' love of decoration could not, of course, fail to appear in their national costumes. Like the *casa maré*, the manner and style of their costume takes

Nadezhda Roshka. Embroidered cushion-covers.

us back to Ancient Rome and to the bas-reliefs of the Trajan Column where the Moldavians' distant ancestors – the Getae-Dacians – are depicted and in whose clothing you may easily detect the main elements of the Moldavians' clothes today: the men's cone-shaped hats, narrow trousers and long belted tunics and the women's blouses with gathered collars and wraparound skirts.

The men's shirts and especially the women's blouses are sumptuously embroidered. The embroidered pattern on the upper part of the sleeves is extraordinarily colourful and bright, and the collars, hem, and main seams of the cut are also

66

embroidered. Some blouses in North Moldavia and Bukovina are embroidered all over. The woven saches edged with a bright broad band on festive occasions are also brightly ornamented. As we have already mentioned, these decorative women's outfits may also be used to decorate the *casa maré* along with the rugs, wall carpets (*peretaré*), cushion-covers (*fatse de perné*), pillow-slips (*moditsé*) and a great many other articles besides.

It is customary for everything to be done in a Moldavian family at a leisurely pace. As soon as a daughter is born, her family starts putting together the dowry

Wall carpet. Fragment.

she will need in twenty years' time. The serious attention traditionally given to all the major events in a person's life such as weddings and birthdays is also particularly apparent in everything concerning a person's final act in life – his death. The funeral rites are therefore extraordinarily beautiful and profoundly symbolic. On the day of the funeral the whole yard, from the house's entrance to the gates, is covered with carpets, cushions and at every crossing on the way to the cemetery the funeral procession stops and lays a carpet as a bridge across the side-street or lane. If the way is short, then two carpets are laid at a time and there are usually twenty-

Moldavian festive costume.

four in all. And each time the last wishes of the deceased are uttered and each carpet is bequeathed to one of the relatives or friends as a bridge, not only across roads but also between the deceased and those who have been left behind on Earth.

When a Moldavian girl marries, she starts weaving these carpets, and they then decorate the *casa maré* along with the rest of her dowry as long as she and her husband are alive. Although still young and energetic, Nadezhda and her husband have already got everything ready for that moment in life which passes nobody by. Everyone wants to leave behind good memories of themselves and so the women weave carpets for their children's weddings and for their own final journey.

But there is also a more joyful custom linked to the Moldavians' handicraft: when a woman borrows a loom from her neighbour, she is supposed to tie all the threads left together as a token of good luck. Unlike most superstitions, this one always comes true — and the hard-working craftswoman of the *casa maré* unfailingly gets good luck.

"I've Got My Own Tower"

By the time I had climbed up to the fifth or sixth floor of the tower, squeezing through the narrow hatches in the ceilings, I had given up counting. But now, at long last, the almost vertical wooden ladders came to an end and overhead I saw the ceiling of this old fortification which had been constructed from huge stone boulders hundreds of years ago. It was cold from the stones and fierce wind whistling through the top floor's narrow loop-holes. Through their uneven-edged blackened slits you could clearly see similar tall fortress towers gleaming white on the hillside. A whole forest of stone watch-towers stretched up towards the sky, vying, as it were, with the mighty pointed snow-white peaks of the Central Caucasus.

The towers tell us much about the grim mountain warriors who built them. You see, I am now in the heart of Upper Svanetia, the most inaccessible part of Georgia, whose impregnable gates have never been penetrated by an enemy, though many attempts were made by Tartar hordes, Tamerlane, the Persians and the Turks. And even earlier, the Svans' martial art and fortitude were well-known to the Romans.

Exactly when and how did it appear – this superb, tall peasant dwelling with massive quarry-stone walls, one and a half metres thick, inside which you could hide from a vendetta and withstand an enemy's siege for long periods of time? The oldest of the Svan towers to have survived are said to be dating from the fourteenth century although, according to ancient sources, they have been in existence in these parts for over two and a half thousand years.

"I've got my own tower," Alexander Djaparidze told me in his house in Mestia, the main settlement of Svanetia. "Nobody lives there any more, mind you, but I still need it, just as my ancestors once did, because it gives me strength. I go inside it whenever I need to think clearly and to feel inner peace. The towers are tributes to our people's past. A lot has disappeared but they're still standing and we take good care of them."

Just as a cloud drifting into the two-peaked Ushba Mountain, which looms over Mestia, stands still, so time in the mountains – the days, years and centuries – are subject to another law from the one in the valleys. It is in no hurry here to write off the past, and the old days live on in present-day customs and traditions. Vestiges of the past are kept in caches behind large creaking doors, which are seldom opened, and then only reluctantly. In the village of Lataly I was highly privileged to be shown a massive silver cross, inlaid with gold, niello and cloisonné medallions of extreme rarity, beauty and value. It had been kept by this family as an heirloom

71

since the 8th century! Before the head of the family died, this treasure was always shown to the eldest son and this tradition had not once been broken for over one thousand and two hundred years.

And not far away in the Church of Taringzel in the village of Pkhotreri I saw a beautifully carved wooden door of the early 11th century. There were six figures of saints in three-dimensional relief with even the folds of their clothing, not to mention their faces, carved in the minutest detail, and a complex, lavish floral pattern. It was obviously the work of a great master for it was namely then that the art of

Mestia. Ancestral towers.

wood-carving, for which the Svans have always been famed, reached its zenith.

In this secluded world everything in the home had to be made by the family from the spoons to the furniture, all the vessels, cupboards, benches, chests for clothing and casks for grain and flour, round tables (*pichki*) and throne-like arm-chairs for the head of the family. On long winter evenings it all used to be carved from well-dried wood and then each square centimetre of surface was decorated with patterns

Mestia—the centre of Svanetia.

73

Alexander Djaparidze.

and designs. As early as the 10th century a Svan craftsman was using not only an axe, saw and pick, but also a chisel, cutter, drill and even a gauge for making patterns. He had an excellent knowledge of wood, of course, and preferred walnut, and knew how to select material which did not flake while being carved. He would then season it for several years at a time.

The road, which has been opened along the River Inguri, has given the mountain people access to many simple, useful and reasonably priced household goods, and in the local department store they may now buy all the bare essentials as well as lux-

Alexander Djaparidze. Wooden vessel,
festive goblets.

ury commodities such as television sets. This being so, you nowadays rarely come across such wonderful carved articles in houses and have to go to museums instead. Even so, the thousand-year-old local arts and crafts are still thriving, I was told at the Local Lore Museum in Mestia, and then taken to Alexander Djaparidze's house.

Alexander was a tall, handsome, middle-aged man. The back door of his house led into his workshop which had everything he needed for his long-standing pastime: a wood lathe, all sorts of cutters and chisels, chocks of red yew-tree, and walnut planks of a colder hue. A post covered all over with carvings would one day be the leg of a Svan arm-chair. "From this round piece here I'm going to make a *katkh* – a ritual goblet which heads of families drink from at festive occasions. From that flat piece I'll make a bowl for soup or yoghurt and from this large one I'll make a two-handled bowl called a *kvanchkh* for vodka," Alexander explained.

When he first started carving twenty-five years ago, many of the old craftsmen were no longer alive and he had no teacher but, to make up for it, many of the cen-

turies-old articles were still intact. It was through them that he learnt the secrets of the craft and got to know the different types of wood and then he went out and found a yew-tree grove seventy-odd kilometres from his village. To start off with, he made simple things, and then more complicated ones, and now he can carve a suite of furniture, utensils and vessels in the Svan style. "I get a lot of orders but I just can't make anything for myself: as soon as people spot a finished arm-chair or table, they just beg me to give it to them and it somehow doesn't seem right to say 'no'," the craftsman said with a smile.

Sure enough, all the furniture in Djaparidze's house is factory-made but all the vessels were made by him, and they are quite splendid! The natural red yew-tree designs in his large polished goblets, vases, salad bowls, dishes, and cups are exquisite.

Alexander Djaparidze grew more and more interested in wood-carving and one day he stopped teaching mathematics and physics at school and took up his favourite subject – handicrafts. He also teaches this intricate craft to young people at the local branch of Solani, the Georgian Association of Folk Arts and Crafts. He was awarded the title of People's Master Craftsman and is a member of the Georgian Artists' Union. The Svans' ancient art is now in good hands.

Not wishing to keep Alexander away from his work, I left him sitting in his yard, intently carving a traditional geometrical pattern on a yew-tree saucer. A mist had rolled out of the valley towards the mountains, the clouds' grey ragged edges were clinging to the tower tops and then drifting along the street and getting entangled in the hawthorn bushes' spiky branches on the convex slope. A cold drizzle set in. The last warm days of autumn were drawing to a close. By evening the heavy clouds would most likely scatter the first snow over this mountainous terrain and the towers' majestic silhouettes would dissolve into the white backcloth of the mountains.

The Art of Ganch

Whenever you see something amazing, you start searching your memory for something else, no matter how vaguely similar that you can compare it to. So, too, in the vast White Hall of Sitorai Makhossa, the country palace of Bukhara Emirs, whose walls are decorated all over with the most exquisite ethereal white lace, which is reflected in the niches' mirrors, the only comparison I could find in the deepest recesses of my memory were Chinese balls with intricately carved ivory designs. Anyone who has not been to Central Asia is hardly likely to know the name of this material – *ganch*.

If one explains what *ganch* is, it may seem highly prosaic: it is neither stone nor clay but something in between – a binding chemical compound rather like alebaster obtained by firing a rock containing gypsum and clay and grinding it into a powder which is then mixed with water and a solution of vegetable glue. It then slowly solidifies as it dries out. The celebrated deceased Uzbek *ganch* craftsman, *usto* * Shirin Muradov from Bukhara, who left behind many pupils, however, used to say that in *ganch* one could convey all the nuances of such human emotions as joy, happiness, hope, sorrow and pain. He was a poet of *ganch* and his "poems" have been bequeathed to his descendants in the decor of the White Hall, a masterpiece created by the young master in 1912-1914, and in the interiors of Tashkent theatres and dozens of other buildings.

Looking back over the long history of this art, we discover that as early as in the 3rd century there was a whole hall of large statues decorated in *ganch* in the Khorezm Palace of Toprak-kal. And in the 5th-7th centuries sculptural compositions in *ganch* on mythological and fairytale themes embellished the Palace of Varakhsha near Bukhara. In the 9th-10th centuries relief carving on flat surfaces became highly popular. We see this in the decor of the Mausoleum of the Samanids in Bukhara and of Khakim at-Termizi in Termez (10th century) and in the palace of the Termez Shahs of the 12th century. Besides depicting lions and griffins, the *ganch* sculptors also went in for geometrical and floral arabesques. By constantly improving their own works, it was namely they who determined the trends of all the subsequent developments in the art of *ganch*.

During its history of many centuries this genre has been enhanced by many dif-

---

* A polite form of address to a master craftsman in Uzbek.– *Ed.*

ferent carving methods or, as they are called by *ganch* sculptors, *pardoz*, and an infinite variety of ornaments. For example, in the White Hall we see both *pakh-pardoz* – carving with a slanting edge inside the relief, *dula-pardoz* – carving with rounded forms, and finally, the old method of *tabaka-pardoz* – delicate flat carving which was perfected by the illustrious sculptor, Shirin Muradov.

A favourite and very effective device used by Muradov was to carve the most intricate lace patterns on mirrors, making them even more beautiful. In this manner he also decorated the Bukhara Hall of the Alisher Navoi Theatre where under his

Tashkent. Former house of Prince Polovtsev.
19th century. Ganch *niche in interior.*
Ganch *pattern on façade.*

supervision all the stylistic variations of *ganch* existent in Uzbekistan were used in a single artistic composition. The best sculptors from all over the republic decorated a series of halls there – the Tashkent, Fergana, Khiva, Samarkand, Termez and, of course, the auditorium itself. The theatre became, as it were, the consummate master's artistic testament.

And for my companion, Makhmud Usmanov, working in this theatre with

79

Shirin Muradov and other experienced masters was like completing his studies at university because he had done all his previous studying under his father, *usto* Usman Ikramov.

"I've been carving *ganch* with my father ever since I was twelve years old," Usmanov recalled. "To start off with, I used to do the preliminary work and then I helped carve my father's patterns and later on I started drawing them myself. In the old days only mosques, madrasahs, the houses of rich landowners and nobles were decorated with *ganch*, and it was only later, in the 18th and 19th centuries, that this art was applied to simple dwellings as well. The masters did not have much work and they were paid a mere pittance for them anyway. My father was a famous *ganch* decorator but we were poor and never had enough money for food and clothing and I barely managed to go to school for six years.

"In the '20s father and I restored old carvings and in 1933 he was invited to work in the republic's Museum of Fine Arts, and for about six months I helped him remove the *ganch* carvings from old houses for an exhibition. In 1940 we set about restoring the Tashkent Museum of Applied Art and in 1943, at the height of the war, the ancient art of *ganch* was destined to experience its renaissance.

"It was at this time that the best *ganch* sculptors were assembled from all over Uzbekistan to decorate the interior of the Mukimi Music Theatre in Tashkent and father and I had the opportunity of working with Shirin Muradov for several years. We also helped him decorate the halls of the Alisher Navoi Theatre."

A true *usto* always has pupils and so, too, does Makhmud: in 1948 he started running *ganch* carving groups for Tashkent schoolchildren, and later on taught at the republic's Benkov Art School.

When, much to everyone's delight, *ganch* started reappearing in architecture in the second half of the '60s, and people once again realised its tremendous decorative potential, *usto* Makhmud was in his prime as an artist. *Ganch*, the oldest decorative art form, did not simply return to people's lives, it experienced a true renaissance, reviving a sparkling array of national designs. Since then Makhmud has decorated the interiors of many public buildings, including the Lenin Memorial in Tashkent.

Not only the art of *ganch* but also its decorators have won recognition. Makhmud Usmanov's great labour has been highly acclaimed and he has been deemed worthy of the title of Merited Arts' Worker and People's Artist of the Uzbek SSR. He has also been awarded state prizes and government orders but if he were asked what he considered his highest award, he would reply without a moment's thought that it is being able to work and make people's lives more beautiful.

"I'm very happy," he often repeated as we walked through sunny Tashkent and he showed me his work. And everywhere we went – to museums, the House of Friendship with Peoples of Foreign Countries, institutions – judging by the reverence with which we were greeted, I realised how much people respected and admired him and how deeply indebted they were to him for his superb gifts.

And then we came to the large new exhibition hall of the Uzbekistan Artists' Union on Lenin Prospekt. Late the previous evening *usto* Makhmud's team of workers had finished decorating a vast panel of the hall and Usmanov wanted me to see it. Although there was still a cold damp smell coming from the drying wall, the scaffolding, splashed with fallen bits of *ganch*, was still standing there, and the floor was smeared with plaster, nothing could detract from the splendour of this vast panel. All one hundred and thirty square metres were covered with a snow-white carved pattern, delicately set off by a cream-coloured background.

With chisel in hand, Makhmud started checking over the masters' work with extreme care but he found everything quite satisfactory. The master, who would soon be celebrating his seventieth birthday, had every reason to be satisfied: the panel's design had been executed by his son, Mirvakhid Usmanov, already an experienced master in his own right, who was following in his father's footsteps.

A special feature of *ganch* is that it dries quickly and so a sculptor cannot work alone, unlike, say, a wood-carver or stonemason: he always has to work with a whole team of pupils if he is to complete the whole work on the damp material in time. Makhmud Usmanov has several such teams and thirty of his hundred and twenty pupils are members of the USSR Artists' Union. One team was now on holiday after completing a large project in Tashkent, another was working in Kishinev, Moldavia, and another two were decorating a memorial to V. I. Lenin and a teahouse in Karshi. Orders are coming in from all over the country and their *ganch* panels now adorn the cities of Moscow, Penza, Donetsk, Kiev, Ivanovo, Sochi and other towns.

"Incisions are made in the concrete slabs to make the layers of *ganch* stick better," Makhmud explained the technique of his work to me. Then the first layer of pure white *ganch* is applied, and when it has dried, a second coloured layer obtained from adding one bucket of dry pigment to five buckets of alebaster, and this layer becomes the background. Then a third layer, also white, from one and a half to two and a half centimetres thick, depending on the kind of pattern and its arrangement is added. This layer we call *khavanda*. The design, the same size as the sketch on paper, is transferred to tracing-paper which is then held up against the wall and the pattern is marked with pin-pricks on the *khavanda*. Then the design's outline is cut along the *ganch* plaster with a sharp chisel and the pattern is cut right through the layer in such a way that the coloured background shows through the gaps. It took a team of forty-two about a month to do this wall, working fourteen hours a day, seven days a week. *Ganch* is a material which has to be worked while it's still pliant, before it's dried out and solidified."

It is an intricate art which takes many years of hard work to master. *Usto* Shirin himself worked and studied under his uncle, the well-known master Khayet, for fif-

Makhmud Usmanov.

teen years before he was deigned worthy of the honorary title of *usto*. You see, it used to be conferred by a council of craft elders after many long years of study. It no longer officially exists but there simply comes a time when the people themselves start calling an artist *usto* and they are never mistaken because such masters as Usmanov really have made a valuable contribution to this old craft.

"In the Alisher Navoi Theatre *usto* Shirin left us examples of all the styles of *ganch* carving," he said. "As you remember, the Khiva ornament consists of circles, the Tashkent ornament has bold deep carvings, the Kokand design and the picture in it is always bordered by a pattern, Bukhara carving is delicate, miniscule and plays on light and shade. In my various projects I have used all these styles and devices." And at once in my mind's eye I saw the most intricate carving intertwined like rose petals in the complex pattern on the ceilings of the V. I. Lenin Memorial Complex, the geometrically concise designs on the ceiling of the House of Friendship, and the large precise Tashkent pattern of vignettes on the walls of the hall here. "Just now," continued the master, "I am elaborating a comprehensive national Uzbek style."

We were sitting at a table in a room decorated with carvings in the sculptor's house in a quiet suburb of Tashkent, sipping green tea from bowls—how else could a conversation take place in the East? And I asked the present-day patriarch of *ganch* about the problems of developing this art in the future.

"Undoubtedly, there are problems," he replied. "The fact is that *ganch* sculptors never used to think of it beyond the building's general structure for *ganch* was always a constructional and functional component of it, organically uniting the structure into an artistic ensemble.

"As a rule, *ganch* carvings were designed in inner rooms and the covered terraces (*aivans*) of reception rooms. Thus, in our traditional structural architecture there were always cornices which the amazingly ingenious *ganch* sculptors decorated with most intricate multi-tiers which acted as transitions from the wall to the flat surface of ceiling in secular buildings or to the dome-shaped vaults in mosques and mausoleums. Usually the vertical *ganch* wall compositions, niches, medallions, and settings were an integral part of the wall's structural articulations. Often the carvings were complemented by stylistically consonant wall-paintings.

"Nowadays, however, *ganch* designs do not always harmonize with the forms and lines of the building or room which it is intended to decorate. In other words, the setting has proved inadequate for the pearl. In houses with entirely different structures, lay-outs, and proportions, *ganch*, though still just as splendid in itself, nevertheless fails to blend with the architecture as it always has, and the sculptor is faced with the task of solving this problem of compatibility. In certain instances sculptors have sufficient good taste to solve this to a great extent but in others,

Makhmud Usmanov. Ganch *pattern in a Moscow hotel.*

they're less successful. They are now boldly experimenting and searching for new ways and I think they'll find them in the end. The huge dimensions of public halls today require larger and much deeper and more embossed patterns, and most likely, simpler and more rhythmic, suppler ones too. As for the designs themselves, I believe that the traditional national ornament has boundless potential to be experimented with. And as far as I can see, my main task is to search for new ways of applying *ganch* without which over a thousand years Central Asian architecture was inconceivable."

Ganch *niche for crockery. Late 19th century.*

Children of a Pagan Muse

The moustachioed sailor had a roughly hewn wooden face, ruddy cheeks, a gawky body and flat planks stuck to his shoulders with wire. From under arched charcoal eyebrows his eyes returned my startled expression as if he was just as puzzled as I was about how this block of wood in a ridiculous-looking tin-can sailor's cap with silver sweet-wrapper buttons on his tunic had come to be at this major All-Union Exhibition of Folk Art in Moscow.

I walked on round the exhibition, stopping by the Caucasian rugs, Ukrainian ceramics, pieces of jewellery from the Baltic republics but soon realised that my thoughts kept stubbornly wandering back to this cheeky-looking sailor and that he was obviously preventing me from concentrating on anything else. So I went back to the figure and suddenly understood I had underestimated it. The sailor no longer appeared so weird: he was simply quite unlike anything else at this exhibition or, in fact, anything else I had ever seen. And although his head was disproportionately large and his arms dangled like a windmill's sails, he now seemed somehow to be well-built and even rather attractive. There was something very daring about the way his designer – and I no longer doubted that the sailor was the work of a skilled master – had carved this engaging fellow without attempting to make him less gawky and more elegant.

Under the figure was a small label where I read: "Scarecrow. Fedor Zhiltsov. Vertlovo village, Borisoglebsky District, Yaroslavl Region." I jotted down the address just in case and about a month later, realising I could not get the sailor off my mind, I wrote Fedor a letter asking him to tell me in more detail about the scarecrows he made and why, where, when and under whom he had studied this craft, and how to find the village if I managed to visit him.

Soon I received a reply. Zhiltsov wrote that he was eighty-two years old and that he had started making scarecrows in about 1960 when he retired. He used to stick them on poles in his vegetable garden to scare away the birds and moles digging holes in his beds. "To start off with," he wrote, "I only made them for that purpose and then just because I liked the look of them. I made them for fun for us old folks and to keep the kiddies amused."

The letter left many of my questions unanswered, and so I set off for Vertlovo which is on the main road from Moscow to Uglich. Fedor Zhiltsov turned out to be a lively and talkative old man and his story, as it were, continued his letter where he had left off. "Little lads used to stare at the figures stuck up in my vegetable garden,

88

and grown-ups, too, used to gape curiously at my unusual scarecrows. Then they started asking me to make them for them, too. Soon there were different-coloured scarecrows on poles flapping their arms about in every yard of our village. Vehicles used to drive past and their drivers would stop and marvel at these strange figures: why, you see, scarecrows in Russia had always been the same – just a pole with rags on it, and sticks for arms and a holey bucket for a head but these looked more like toys!

So they'd get out of their vehicles, come up closer to the fence, shake their heads

Fedor Zhiltsov. Scarecrows.

and stare and then ask for one. And children are always asking me to make them a scarecrow.

"Well, I says, I'll make you one if you get top marks at school. Show me your report and you'll get a scarecrow. So one of them brought me his report book and took his present and kept giggling. 'What are you giggling about?' I asked. 'Oh, I've cheated you, Uncle Fedya. That report book isn't mine. I'll never get more than seven out of ten but I wanted a scarecrow so much!' 'Well,' I says, 'at least you owned up.' The little lads help me out by bringing me shiny sweet wrappers for the buttons, cartridge belts, old medals, and tin cans for peaked caps – you see, nearly all my scarecrows are soldiers. I make them from memory. I've fought in three wars myself – World War I, our Civil War and World War II. And I've got orders and medals to prove it. So, now I'm carving soldiers.

"I was born in the village of Chukholda and lived there until I was eleven. My dad was a peasant. There was eight of us children and I was the oldest. When I was eleven I was sent to work as a labourer for a merchant in Kronshtadt. I worked for him for eight years. It was there, in 1910, in front of someone's house that I saw a

painted scarecrow rather like the ones I'm making now: it served him as a sort of household god and ensured there was peace and quiet in his home. But why are we talking about the scarecrows indoors, let's go outside and I'll show them to you."

Evening was drawing near and the sun was shining dimly from under the edges of a mauve storm-cloud drifting from the west, and you could feel rain was on its way. The wind was only just stealing up to the village along with a thunderstorm but an occasional gust was already sweeping through it and when we went out into the vegetable garden, about three dozen scarecrows greeted us with a friendly wave of their winged arms, accompanied by a loud whining sound caused by wire scraping against wood. The regiment of scarecrow soldiers was led by a tough-looking, blue-

Fedor Zhiltsov.

eyed fellow standing to attention right in the corner of the fence, flapping his blue wings and staring boldly up at the tense sky. The soldiers were wearing excellently "tailored" khaki uniforms made of slightly darkened alder bark, and fully kitted out with cartridge belts and shiny medals. Five dashing lads in uniforms were supporting their commanding officer from behind and in the heart of the garden stood the veterans, flapping their arms. After ten to fifteen years of service all year round in open air they had shed their smart uniforms, and lost the paint off their faces and their dapper curling moustaches, and only cracked old grey wood was left. Then all of a sudden I spotted a silvery blue dress among the grey soldiers.

"That's my wife – Taisia - I've made one of her, too. I was twenty-nine when we married and we've been together for fifty-three years. We didn't celebrate our golden wedding anniversary, mind you, but we get on grandly. We've three sons, one daughter, nine grandchildren and one great-grandson. I made one of her when she was seriously ill not long ago. We're old folks now and anything might happen to us. Last winter I got very sick too and reckoned I'd had it. But then spring came and it grew warmer and I rallied round. And as soon as I'd got a bit stronger, I carved one of me in alder over there – see that soldier.

"Mind you, I've started making less of them now because I'm not so strong as I used to be. It might not seem hard work – I only use three tools – a saw, an axe and a knife but while you're carving one, you get as worn out as if you'd chopped up a whole stack of logs."

As though understanding that we were talking about them, the scarecrows started fluttering and whirring, and a greyish-blue storm-cloud swept down over the village like a marauder, a short squall shook the air and large drops of rain started falling on the ground. We went inside where Fedor's wife had already heated up the samovar. I looked back at the scarecrows from the porch. The dashing young soldier in a green tunic and his young wife in a blue dress were waving to each other, and warding off danger from the house, and they must have been doing a good job if the old couple had lived together in peace, love and harmony for fifty-three years.

And, you know, Zhiltsov's scarecrows, especially the grey wrinkled ones, are very similar to the wooden images which were found at Charozero by people from the Cherepovetsk Museum, Vologda district, which, in keeping with an ancient custom, depicted the master and mistress of the house and stood in exactly the same manner on the estate. And wooden images of communal and household gods were often kept by Eastern Slavs in the remote past: in a chronicle story of 983 a Christian Varangian recorded that the idols were made of wood with an axe and knife.

But why did I suddenly recall this? Was I really beginning to think that it was one and the same pagan muse who had inspired the carvers of the post sculptures at Charozero, and then hundreds of years later, the carver of the wooden figures in Kronshtadt and not so long ago, Uncle Fedya when he had started carving fancy scarecrows and scaring the birds off the branches in Vertlovo?

Time out
of Mind

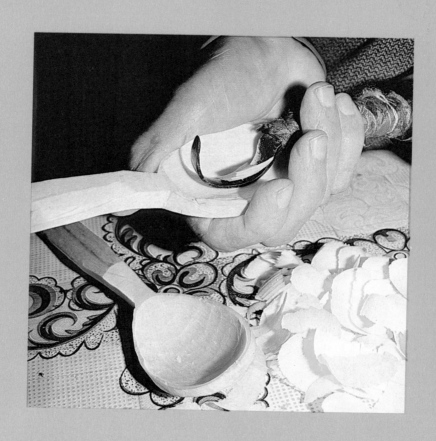

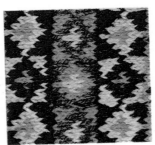

At Marfa's House on the Pechora

Ust-Tsilma is not completely buried in the wild northern forests: it is, of course, a long way off, and can only be reached by boat along the River Pechora and by air but you can still get there in a day from Moscow by changing planes at Syktyvkar. And you can't call the village a god-forsaken backwater either because its hundred-year-old two-storey boarded cottages painted in bright colours certainly do not look neglected. Even so, among all other Russian villages this one is quite unique, and there is much more to it than meets the eye. It is traditionally held that the village was founded in the mid-16th century by the Novgorodians when they were assimilating new hunting forests and lands. Later on serfs fled here in search of freedom, and Old Believers sought refuge from persecution here in the dense taiga, bringing precious old books with them. They fished, hunted, and tilled the land. So the centuries passed, reaping changes in people's lives but the old traditions were not forgotten.

A great many songs, folktales and epics have been recorded by researchers in these parts; over a thousand old manuscripts have been transferred to Moscow and Leningrad; many museums have fine collections of old embroidery, wooden carvings, peasant utensils, needlework and knitting from here. But only in Ust-Tsilma can you still see the *Gorka* folk festival with its round dances and traditional costumes.

"Tiranova's the person for you – go and see Tiranova," the villagers advised me on hearing that I was interested in folk artists. "She's our best craftswoman, and the one who leads all our songs and dances – our 'universal godmother', as we used to say in the old days."

Marfa Tiranova's sturdy, austere and proud-looking house suited her perfectly and paid tribute to her. It loomed over the gently-sloping riverbank like a two-storey boulder with six windows. During its hundred years of service the unpainted house had turned a mellow dark-brown – its logs could get no darker, and its white platbands gave it consonance with the present without depriving it of dignity.

Does Fate deal its cruellest blows on the best and strongest people because it knows that they'll withstand them? On no other house in the village, which stretched for a good five kilometres along the riverbank, did I see a memorial plaque with four names under a red star. On nearly every other house there were one, two or three of these tragic reminders of the grief inflicted by the last war but

Marfa Tiranova.

only here did I read: "Yegor Ivanovich Nosov; Fedor Ivanovich Nosov; Sergei Ivanovich Nosov; Mikhail Ivanovich Nosov."

"My eldest, Yegor, only managed to stay alive for eight months after the war broke out. It brought us a lot of suffering, it did. In our family we lost two brothers and an uncle, my aunt's husband and our neighbour lost her father and son. Ten people in three houses," Marfa said with a heavy sigh. "When the war ended, I remarried. It's a wise man who calls but a foolish woman who follows, as we used to say. Nothing good came of it, and we were never happy. And not long ago my

Marfa Tiranova. Knitted mittens and stockings.

son died – cancer killed him off in two months. And then my sister died, and soon afterwards, my best friend. So I haven't taken part in our festival for five years now."

She suddenly started singing a happy little song, thinking it impolite to burden me with her sorrows. Then she energetically pushed the spinning-wheel and wool to one side and disappeared behind the stove. Soon afterwards there came a delicious aroma of potatoes and fried onions and in a trice a frying-pan of sweet-smelling potatoes, boiled fish, a samovar and jam appeared on the table. In the course of our

97

lively conversation Marfa told me that almost everyone in their village knitted and spun but only in winter because there was plenty of other work to be done in the spring, summer and autumn. "My mother and grandmother used to knit patterned gloves and stockings. You see, we wore box-calf boots and not bast shoes, and we used to make leather soles for our patterned stockings and stick heels to them and then stick nails in them so they made a noise when we danced. And we used to tuck our trousers into our stockings and instead of pulling them up to our knees, we used to wear our stockings puckered because they looked prettier that way. And we

After 16th-century fashion.

used to knit the men's socks with patterns all over, while we women usually wore black or navy-blue ones with strips at the top.

"We used to dye the wool three colours with young birch leaves – red, green and yellow – and then mix them to get other shades.

"I'm knitting mittens now. Last winter I made thirty-two pairs and not one's left. I get orders from all over the country, including Moscow.

"But why have you had so little to eat? Help yourself to more potatoes – this is the best spoon – my late husband, Semion Savvich made it like a ladle."

"Marfa Nikolayevna, if we're not going to see you at the festival, will you please put on your festive costume here in your home because, you know, legends are told about it."

"Oh well, if you really do insist..." The old lock on the trunk made the twanging sound you'd expect, the lid creaked open and the clean and shiny room was suddenly ablaze with gold, lilac, dark-green and blue as brocades, satins, embroidered dresses, shawls and intricate silver belts came showering out. Sarafans after sarafans, each for a set occasion – one for visiting in, another, too, only on special occa-

sions, yet another even smarter one, over a hundred years old, from her mother for weddings or christenings, another simpler one for everyday wear, yet another beautiful one for parties and, at last, the most beautiful one of all, for the *Gorka* festival. I had already seen sarafans in Ust-Tsilma because elderly women wear them even on ordinary week-days and the several starched slips they wear underneath make their figures even more stately. But I had not seen any festive costumes like these before. Shall I attempt to describe them? No, I think I'll leave that up to the photographs. But when a flushed Marfa Nikolayevna glided grandly out from behind the screen in a pistachio-golden silk sarafan and a dark-blue reps scarf with bright orange splashes, I was completely dumbstruck. In these striking clothes her beauti-

99

ful kind face became stern and solemn. Nikolai Onchukov, a collector of folk epics, was indeed right when he wrote at the beginning of the century that in the local traditional dress in the Pechora region lingered traces of Old Russian boyars' brocade, the like of which in the centre of Russia you could only see in museums. And it's not just that they've carefully preserved fashions dating back to Ivan the Terrible's time in trunks and chests of drawers, but, it's that they've kept the fashions alive! Many of the outfits were not inherited from mothers and grandmothers but sewn quite recently by local dressmakers at home in keeping with all the traditions.

The silks and brocades and shiny gold gave one a thrilling glimpse of the coming festival, and I could tell that in her mind's eye Marfa was also seeing the dances and songs she had taken part in before dawn in the past. How many festivals she had conducted in the past and what authority she now enjoyed over the festivals and people! Short, even small, one could say, but stately, broad-boned and sparkling-eyed, she would say something ever so quickly to her old women friends and they would catch her meaning at once, and everything would go smoothly. The next morning they would sing and dance at the festival without her but the morning after she would be going out with the rest of the villagers to mow hay for it is July, the height of the mowing-season in the Pechora's meadows.

The Spoon-maker

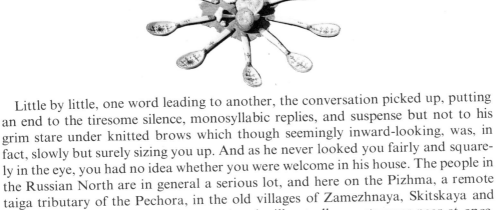

Little by little, one word leading to another, the conversation picked up, putting an end to the tiresome silence, monosyllabic replies, and suspense but not to his grim stare under knitted brows which though seemingly inward-looking, was, in fact, slowly but surely sizing you up. And as he never looked you fairly and square-ly in the eye, you had no idea whether you were welcome in his house. The people in the Russian North are in general a serious lot, and here on the Pizhma, a remote taiga tributary of the Pechora, in the old villages of Zamezhnaya, Skitskaya and Zagrivochnaya, they are very reserved and will not allow a stranger near at once. They'll keep on their guard until they are sure that the newcomer is genuinely inter-ested in their way of life and for the right reasons. Harsh times and isolated way of life could not help but leave traces on character and customs of these people.

I decided in Ust-Tsilma to get here: my mind was made up as soon as I caught sight of the wonderful painted wooden Pizhma spoons during the meal at Marfa Tiranova's and found out that in the whole area they were now only made by Gri-gory Chuprov of Zamezhnaya. By local standards this was quite near, just only a half-hour away by plane. Not so long ago, however, before there were planes and motor-boats, it would have taken two days to get here, riding upriver over the rapids, one of which had earned the name "Bandit" for its ill repute.

Raskolniki, as the dissenters from the Russian Orthodox Church were known, were drawn to these remote and isolated lands and by the beginning of the 18th cen-tury an Old Believers' monastery was established here. The Old Believers staunchly upheld the old customs and traditions not only in their religious practice but in their everyday lives, too.

And the Pizhma turned out to be a sumptuous treasure-trove of folk talent where highly valuable materials had been collected by archeographers, folklore specialists and art historians. The village of Avraamovskaya, for instance, was famous for its epic storytellers, Zamezhnaya for its songs and as the centre of the spoon industry which, until recently, had supplied the whole district with spoons. These golden spoons, which shine in the light like opals and still have the oldest shape and tradi-tional design in Russia, are light and elegant and have always been preferred to alu-minium or stainless steel ones. However, there are very few of them left nowadays and that is why they are treasured in the village and only brought out for guests and on special occasions.

...The plane flew over the taiga and down below the Pizhma, the most beautiful tributary of the Pechora, sparkled in the sunlight as it meandered through a green carpet. All of a sudden the green hues changed slightly as the dark salad-coloured speck of a meadow appeared between the dark conifers, and the plane dived into this gap, the golden sand-banks flashed by and it was soon bouncing along the grass. And as soon as the sound of its whirring engine died away, the passengers came out into a world of chirring crickets and dragonflies.

The village was on the other side of the river, and as you walked across the bridge, the rapid current of crystal-clear water, pressing the reeds down to the bottom, made you dizzy and you involuntarily clung on tighter to the vacillating wooden railings.

In his young days Grigori Chuprov had been a Jack-of-all-trades: he had made excellent men's and women's footwear, and birchbark vessels with red painted designs on a green background. He started carving spoons in 1946 after misfortune had struck him. After undergoing three operations, he had lost a leg and returned from the war on crutches.

"Now I'm the only spoon-maker left, but there used to be lots in the village," said Grigory, stroking his thick grey beard and running his hand through his grey hair. Then he buttoned the collar of one of his best shirts he had put on because it was one of those lovely warm sunny days when he could sit and relax on the mound of earth running round the walls of his house and warm his aching old wounds. And then, giving in to my entreaties, he set off towards the shed, leaning on my shoulder.

The cool damp air inside smelled of fresh wood shavings, resin and drying firewood. Chuprov selected a metre-long birch log and asked me to put it on the saw-horse. With a large well-set, two-handled saw we then sawed off a block about twenty centimetres long, the length of a spoon, and Chuprov skilfully chopped it into four equal lengths with his axe. Next he put the chock on a log and started squaring it with the axe, first cutting off the two bottom edges obliquely with strong precise blows until the handle began to form and then turning the chock, rounded off the edges at the other end, scraping off the excess wood on the back and in less than five minutes the chock had quickly shrunk in his hands and taken on the rough shape of a spoon. Then the craftsman plunged the axe into the log, picked up an ordinary knife and rounded off the spoon with it. Then he worked at it with a chisel and put it down to dry. Afterwards he would scrape its rough surface smooth and paint it. We went back to his house for this crucial part of the work and he sat down comfortably at the table, put his spoons and simple work tools down on the oilcloth in front of him, mixed the red and green water colours with resin in small jars, opened a small bottle of Indian ink, held his nib up to the light to check it was free of hairs, wiped it with a rag just in case, dipped it into the ink and gently touching the wood, drew the first tiny, slightly blurred diamond. Then he drew a cross inside it, dividing it in four and in each part drew a circle with squiggly lines or crowns on top rather like those on a chess queen. Then he ran his nib over the

Bridge over River Pizhma.

smooth surface, making crosses, diamonds, meanders, loops, curls, ovals and dots, ancient symbols of a forgotten cult which scientists have deciphered as signs of birds, nests, hatched eggs, fledglings, and of the spring awakening of nature, fertility, goodness, happiness and well-being. The same design soon appeared on the back of the spoon as well but it was in fact different because the same design is never repeated on both sides of a spoon. And you will never find a craftsman making two spoons with exactly the same shape or design because stereotypes are taboo here and each spoon is a true work of art.

Chuprov painted the patterns in red ochre and green and then gave his composition a crimson border and the rather stark, concise and symmetrical ornament shone gaily on the white spoon. Although you won't find a similar pattern anywhere else, there is still something very familiar about the signs. Why, of course! They're very like the headpieces and initials of the old manuscripts which this area abounds in! An ancient stratum of highly sophisticated northern Russian art lives on in the old craftsman's spoons. And, what's more, they are practical utensils in daily life and not just beautiful museum objects.

Grigory Chuprov. Spoons.

"You haven't any finished ones by chance, Grigory?" a woman called from the passageway, "I'd take a dozen: my children have come home for the holidays and my old ones have completely had it." It was one of his neighbours.

The craftsman reluctantly tore himself away from his work and called to his sister who had gone off to feed the poultry, "Agafya, have a look in the dresser, will you!" Agafya wrapped several new golden spoons in newspaper and the neighbour went away satisfied.

Grigory Chuprov.

I lifted a painted spoon up to my mouth to see how convenient it was for eating with. It was as light as a feather, elegant, a noble oval shape, like old Russian spoons, flat on top and slightly curved at the bottom of its handle. It lay lightly and comfortably between your fingers, and its elongated tip felt pleasantly warm on your lips. No, you wouldn't burn your mouth supping with this!

"It's too early to try it out yet – if you sit down to eat with this, you'll eat paint with your soup," said the craftsman with a grin. "I've still got to varnish it. We used to use hempseed oil, excellent it was, but now the oil's worse but it'll still do."

Grigory dipped his wood-grouse quill into the thick dark fluid and coated the spoon with it. Just as magically as if Midas had touched it, the plain birch spoon suddenly turned to gold.

"Bright water" is the name of the old Russian town, Vologda, in translation from one of the languages of the Ugro-Finnish tribe who once lived there. And as clear and bright as pure northern snow is the superb Russian art of Vologda bobbin, or pillow, lace. Today its pattern—a linen snowflake—is the town's symbol.

...The wooden bobbins clicked away gently and melodiously in Anna Gruzdeva's hands. No matter how hard I tried, I could not follow or catch a sequence in the flashing movements of this hereditary Vologda lace-maker's fingers. And no wonder, for, you see, lace-making, is no simple craft and takes many years to learn. Seventy-eight-year-old Anna Gruzdeva, for instance, has been making lace for seventy-two years. The sources of this wonderful folk craft may be traced back to the remote past. An Ipatievskaya Chronicle of 1252 describes the robes of Grand Prince Daniil Galitsky as being "decorated with golden lace". And at the end of the 16th century the Moscow tsar presented the wife of the Siberian Khan Kuchum with a fur-coat "trimmed with silver-threaded satin, a lace collar, silver-threaded black silk and coral buttons".

So, lace must have been highly esteemed in the past if tsars and princes wore it. Indeed, until the 18th century it was a sign of wealth and luxury in as far as it was made of gold and silver threads or fine gold string and was used for the most part to embellish royal, boyar, ecclesiastical robes, frequently in combination with gold embroidery. The tsars, boyars and richest merchants used to have their own clothiers. The consummate lace-makers of Tsaritsa Maria Ilyinichna (mid-17th century), *boyar* Golitsin and the Stroganov merchants of Solvychegodsk are renowned. In 18th-century Russian portraits we see gold- and silver-threaded shawls and capes whose patterns usually consist of a rhythmical series of circles alternating with floral motifs or fan-shaped designs. In the 18th century, white lace was made by serf girls on landowners' estates and at the end of the 18th and beginning of the 19th century large lace-making factories opened which were worked entirely by serfs. Lace-making gradually spread to towns and villages and was used to decorate wedding sheets, towels, curtains and clothes.

Lace was made in many parts of Russia, especially in the north and on the Volga where flax was grown. In the 19th century there were twelve lace-making centres in Russia but the real heart of this craft was Vologda. At one time it was practically impossible to find a cottage in the town or a neighbouring village where people did not make lace on the long winter evenings. What's more, this craft was a great sup-

Anna Gruzdeva.

Vologda lace.

port to the peasant economy. The secrets or, rather, technique, as there is only one, were handed down from one generation to another and from mother to daughter but aptitude for this most intricate art and talent for creating pictures and patterns of ones own was something one was born with... It is not for nothing that the word "lace" figures in many Russian sayings and proverbs to do with people's skill.

Fortunately, this folk art has stood the test of time and managed not only to compete with complex lace-making machines but also to prove yet again that no machine can match a skilled pair of hands. Lace-makers' crafts are run in Vologda,

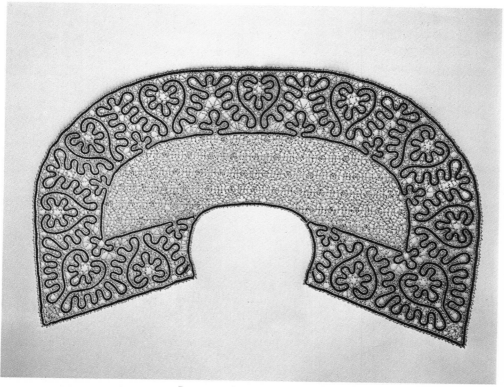

Lace with metal threads.

Yelets, Kirov and Mikhailovo near Ryazan. Each region has its own style and pattern. Vologda lace-makers like to make the main pattern contrast sharply with a light intricate background. Kirov lace-makers prefer folial ornaments and Yelets laces are the lightest and finest.

The Vologda *Snezhinka* * Craft has over six thousand lace-makers working from home and over a hundred in their workshops. Four hundred different types of lace

* *snezhinka* – a snowflake.– *Tr*.

110

are made – in the old days you would hardly have found such a selection at any market. Their articles range from snowflake-shaped serviettes to huge exhibition curtains, bed-covers and panels. Every year no less than thirty of them are sent from Vologda to various exhibitions around the country and abroad. And prizes and awards arrive annually from the twenty international fairs and exhibitions. The Grand Prix of the 1937 World Exhibition and Gold Medal of the 1957 Brussels World Exhibition are among the prizes on display in the Craft's museum.

The senior lace-makers' skill and experience are greatly valued here: every year the professional technical school attached to the craft turns out eighty to ninety lace-makers, holds competitions for new patterns and organises study groups. Lace-making, just like any other craft, has its prodigies such as Anna Gruzdeva.

I had no problem finding her flat. I had expected to see intricate carvings on the window frames, which many Vologda cottages still boast but several years ago Anna was given a flat with all modern conveniences in a new high-rise. And although she had retired long ago and her grandsons were already grown-up with children of their own, and her eyesight was not as good as it had been, she could not possibly give up her work. A person never gives up his craft and his life's main work to the very end and it's been like this here time out of mind. In Anna's room three pillows, one bigger than the other, are piled on trestles and a tight roll of lace patterns is stacked on top of a cupboard. "I haven't thrown a single one out all these years," she told me.

Lace-makers produce just about anything you can think of – waistcoats, cardigans, scarfs, serviettes, collars and shawls. Lavsan is now used to make lace instead of satin and silk, but the technique and patterns created in the wooded north are still similar to those the peasants used to decorate their porches and platbands with hundreds of years ago. Obviously, long ago everything was tested out so thoroughly in this most intricate art that you're bound to go wrong if you try anything slightly different.

While she talked, Anna's hands kept working away as if of their own accord. Hanging from pins on the pillows were forty pairs of light wooden bobbins on white threads which she was sorting out and plaiting so quickly, it was difficult to see how, and then fastening the flax thread to the edges of the design with pins. And as the bobbins melodiously clicked away, a plaited thread ran along the design from pin to pin, forming, like in a cobweb, row upon row of new little squares, triangles and corners. These were snowflakes with the lovely creative folk designs we knew so well.

"Why, this is just a simple pattern but when we're making something for an exhibition, sometimes as many as thirty of us sit down with eighty pairs of bobbins each. And we'll spend a whole month making a bed-cover measuring three metres square. This sort of work's a joy to look at. What I love most is making white lace – the linen's beautiful in itself. We're not the first to make lace and we won't be the last either: I've already hung bobbins over my little three-year-old great-granddaughter's bed as mascots, and, who knows, perhaps they'll come in handy, too..."

Once upon a time in a village there lived Bogunchikha,
Who knitted shawls, one more lovely than the other.
And her friends started asking her
To show them how she made her beautiful cobwebs.
But Bogunchikha did not want to share her secret
And that's most likely why her shawls started turning out
worse and worse.
And soon everyone forgot all about Bogunchikha.

Fact or fiction, this is what the needlewomen in Orenburg villages tell anyone who comes to find out about their old craft. None of this region's best knitters keeps secrets from each other or from their visitors. All their art is on display and they have nothing to hide and all you need is a good pair of eyes, a good memory and nimble hands and then everything will turn out as well as can be. That is, of course, if you start knitting when you're still a child and spend your whole life doing it.

Fardana Shafikova, for instance, from the old Cossack village of Zholtoye, founded in 1825, has been knitting all her life. Here, around the town of Saraktash, a cluster of villages famous for their skilled knitters was formed long ago.

"Strictly speaking, there's no secret at all to our art," she told me, after first giving me a traditional cup of tea with cream to warm me up when I came in from the frost. "Knitting's done the same way the world over and the choice of patterns for a scarf or cape is much the same, too. You make tiny holes, some bigger than others in alternate rows, and you get ever-such a lot of patterns from them! And we all learn to knit when we're very small, and it's passed on from mother to daughter."

...In its present form the Orenburg knitting industry was started up by the Cossacks over two hundred years ago, in the second half of the 18th century, joining together two older crafts. One of the predecessors of the fluffy shawl with its cobweb pattern was the thermal Kalmyk or Cossack shawl, which was worn under light clothing in fierce frosts, and knitted in plain stitch from the softest goats' fleece. The other was the fine lace shawls made by Ural Cossack women. From the first the Orenburg fluffy shawl, which knitters will run through a wedding ring to impress you even more, inherited its quality for retaining heat and from the second, lightness, delicacy and beauty.

There really do seem to be no particular secrets to the art so why is it that when you put what seems like a beautifully-knitted shawl next to one made by Fardana

Shafikova or one of the other best Orenburg knitters, the former immediately dimmed in comparison? And, if all the shawls are identical, why is it that Fardana was given the honorary title of "Senior Master" and sent a diploma from the USSR Academy of Arts "for preserving and developing the craft of knitted shawls with traditional lacy 'cobweb' patterns and for creating highly artistic new models"?

"Well, would you like to see a fluffy shawl being made right from the start?" asked Fardana, picking up a little bundle containing some combed yellowish Orenburg goats' fluff which looked more like tow.

"First, we remove all the hairs and bits from the fluff," Fardana explained, pulling a tuft of fluff out of the large ball and setting to work. As always, her sixteen-year-old daughter just back from school was helping her. Six-year-old Rita also helped her mother a lot but that day she had hurt her arm badly and wiping her tears away was silently watching her elders. It is quite laborious and, frankly, tedious work pulling out all the thistles, seeds and blades of grass stuck in the fluff but it has to be done and, what's more, only by hand.

"Now the fluff has to be carded," said Fardana when all the noticeable bits had been pulled out of the fluff. She clamped the wooden base of the comb between her knees. It had two rows of sharp needle-length steel teeth, closely fitted together. She ran the fluff through it several times, removing the short fibres, and then washed it in soapy water and when it was dry, combed it through again several times. Now it was much lighter, silkier to touch and shinier.

Next came a very important stage: the shapeless ball of fluff was gradually spun into very fine, even thread. This required much experience. Fardana turned the spindle with one hand while gently moving the strain of fluff, as fine as a trickle of sand in an hour-glass, with the fingers of her other hand and out came a very delicate yarn of wool. To make it tougher and more resilient, Fardana and her daughter then joined the fluffy thread to a shiny silk thread by twining them together between their thumbs and index fingers. Then they wound it into a ball. Now the yarn was ready to be knitted.

The knitter's skill, of course, accounts for much but the quality of the fluff is no less important. It is the icy wind, roaming freely across the Orenburg steppes in winter and the dry air of the sharply continental plain that facilitates the growth of a soft thick lining under the goats' coats which is combed out in February and March. And it is for this reason that the industry could not be developed anywhere else for that matter. And you can't say attempts have not been made to breed this capricious strain of goats elsewhere.

As long ago as 1818 a French professor of Oriental studies by the name of Jubert bought a vast herd of 1,300 goats, and had it driven from the steppes to Odessa and then shipped to Marseilles. No matter where they tried to graze these unique Orenburg goats – in France, England and later on in the New World – after a few seasons they turned into ordinary coarse-haired goats and lost their fluffy linings forever.

In the whole world the Orenburg goat has only one rival – the wild Tibetan Kashmir goat, a related strain whose wonderful fluffy coats won fame in Europe as early

Fardana Shafikova and her daughter, Rimma.

as in the 17th century. And among the various wonders on sale in America's famous Niemann Marcus Store, buyers are offered dresses made from the most expensive material in the world – cashmere, woven from the fluff of the Tibetan goat which is collected from the steep mountain slopes of Hindu Kush during the animals' moulting season.

Many experts, however, consider that the less exotic fluff of the Orenburg goat is of a better quality than that of its Tibetan relative, and the worldwide demand for these cobweb-patterned shawls and scarfs has not slackened for two centuries. At

Festive shawl.

the beginning of the 19th century the English firm, Lipner, even put out a large number of imitation Orenburg scarves.

There are five goat-breeding state farms in the Orenburg district and the largest is the Guberlinsky Pedigree State Farm located in the Guberlinsky Mountains. There is so much snow here in winter that you can not get to the central part of the estate, let alone to the herds dotted about. The goatherds' job is therefore not easy for they have to graze and feed the livestock, keep a close watch on their rations to ensure they grow good fluffy coats in the autumn, guard them against wolves, see the

8*

breeding rate is high and not miss the moment when the goats start rubbing against the rocks and fences when it is time to comb out the fluff. All the goats have to be combed while the fluff is new. Although no more than half a kilogram is taken from each goat, a goatherd can only see to about a dozen animals a day.

To look at, the Orenburg goat seems just like any other goat. It is frisky, of medium height, with a greyish-brown coat and twisted horns. If you did not know about its marvellous fluff, you certainly would not guess about it. Time out of mind goat-breeders have dreamed of rearing white goats. Its fluff does not need bleaching, thus removing the most hard and time-consuming part of the work, and the gossamer scarfs made from it are simply magnificent. The number of white goats is on the increase and in time they will most likely supplant their greyish-brown fellows, bringing even greater fame to the old craft...

By now the ball of wool in Fardana's hands has grown to the size of a large orange, and she has picked up two fine knitting needles with black rubber stoppers to keep the stitches on at the ends. After learning from her that to make a shawl one and a half metres wide you have to knit a row of four hundred stitches, I was very surprised the needles were only twenty-five to thirty centimetres long. "What do you expect – it's only fluff," laughed Fardana, "so it doesn't take up much space and on this needle you can knit up to five hundred stitches.

"There's going to be a five-circle pattern on this shawl," she continued. "And in each circle there'll be five diamonds. To help me remember the pattern more easily, I mentally divide the whole surface into four equal squares. And when I've knitted the central pattern, I knit on the band and border which I've made separately. One shawl takes at least a week to knit and then it has to be carefully washed in bleach and dried on a special frame. And then it'll look like this one." She removed a small bundle from a cupboard and a snow-white cloud came streaming out. It belonged to her daughter, Rimma, and I took a photograph of her in it in the snow in front of the house.

Why Flowers Never Fade in Zhostovo

Before applying the first dab with his brush, Dmitry Kledov carefully looked over the round tray, stroked its black lacquered surface with his palm as usual to make sure it was perfectly polished and dust-free. In his mind's eye he ran the top of his brush over the tray's top to get a better feel of the space the design was to fill, and then with confident rotatory movements drew a pink heart near the centre with his soft squirrel brush. And after he had added five petals, a rose, which was to be in the centre of the bouquet, burst into bloom on the metal tray. Using the same paint, the artist drew another, slightly smaller rose nearby, and then yet another, and two tender buds a little nearer to the edge of the tray. "My favourite flowers are white and pink," he said.

Zhostovo is a village with green back-yards, wooden houses with carved window platbands, a grassy bank sloping gently down to the river, a pale-blue sky, creamy clouds, and a gleaming dark-blue forest in the distance... In a word, with all the pastel shades of a central Russian landscape. Nothing, it seems, jars with this peaceful and soothing colour scheme. However, while walking through the village, you see clusters of rowanberries blazing among the orchards, bright crimson dahlias in the front gardens and a bush of golden chrysanthemums shining like little suns in front of a cottage's window. These bold fiery colours and this sharp contrast of exotic hues are splashed about nature's pastel canvas. And how perfectly they are captured by the folk artists of this village near Moscow in one of the most exuberant forms of Russian applied folk art, illustrious Zhostovo hand-painted laquered metal trays, which has flourished for over a hundred and fifty years!

The painted trays first appeared in Russia at the end of the 18th century, in St. Petersburg and the Urals, and in 1825 a craft with its own style of painting emerged in the village of Zhostovo, forty kilometres from Moscow. The traditional techniques of preparing the material and lacquer on the metal trays, once forged and now mostly stamped, are still in current use. There are now dozens of artists working in Zhostovo, many of whom are from the Kledov family who have been making trays from the very start. The head of the family is sixty-eight-year-old Dmitry Kledov. Hanging on a wall of his house is an old tray painted at the beginning of the century by his father and depicting an idyllically joyful scene of some hunters in a boat, mountains, sun, the river and a flock of birds. You won't see another like it because these days the trays are decorated almost exclusively with bouquets of flowers. The works of his uncle, Nikita Kledov, were awarded prizes at the 1937 World Exhibition in Paris. Dmitry has also won many prizes himself, and his nephew, Victor Kledov, and his wife, Zoya Kledova, are also outstanding artists. There are many other artists in the family as well – Zinaida Platonova, Lidia Vosareva, Raissa Kledova, and they are all Dmitry's pupils.

"I started helping my father at work when I was twelve," Dmitry Kledov told me. "To start off with, I worked at the Vishnyakov Brothers' and then Andrei Volgin's workshops and then at fifteen I became free-lance. And I've worked solidly at it for over fifty years except for the four years of war when I was at the front. At

Dmitry Kledov (the elder). Tray. Early 20th century.

first, I used to work at home but when construction work on a factory began in Zhostovo in 1929, I started helping them carry the bricks because, you see, I had my own horse. Now I work at home again – I'm beginning to feel my age."

After turning the tray round on his lap – he was holding his metal "canvas" just like they used to in the old days – and making sure the picture looked well from all angles, Kledov started adding new flowers to the roses which would form a bou-

Modern Zhostovo tray. Fragment.

118

Dmitry Kledov.

quet with them; with confident strokes of red paint he drew dahlias, delicate blue forget-me-nots and violet pansies.

He knew perfectly well that the bouquet had to look like an integral whole and had not to be weighed down by unnecessary details and that the harmonious composition of the picture in the centre of the tray had not to be spoiled by excessively bright splashes of colour. All this required exceptional sensitivity and precision of the artist. At last he had drawn the last modest daisy and set to filling the black spaces between the flowers with bright green leaves, stems and grass.

Modern Zhostovo tray.

And now the bouquet was finished and not even a blade of grass needed to be added but it was still not quite ready for though it had been marked out and the flowers drawn in, it had still to be instilled with life. This wonderful awakening came about as soon as the artist drew in the shadows of the petals, leaves and stems with a very fine brush. Why, the flowers sprang to life before your very eyes. The bouquet grew lighter from the densely painted centre to the edges, and the black background gradually increased until it finally filled the whole surface of the tray. The bouquet then seemed to be suspended in the centre. The first stage of the work

121

was complete and the tray was put away in a drying cupboard for the night.

Next morning when Dmitry picked up his tray again and gave it a fresh look, the colours had soaked in and slightly lost their gloss. So he wiped the tray with an oily cloth and made them sparkle just as brightly as before. Then he applied broad splashes of semi-transparent red, dark-blue and green paint to the bouquet all over, casually catching the tips of the petals and leaves, highlighting the hearts of the flowers, livening up the green leaves and balancing the cold and warm tones.

During this second stage the flowers became luscious and acquired body, as it were.

In the two final traditional stages of painting Zhostovo trays, whiting highlights are applied to the petals, giving the flowers a semi-magical quality, and the leaves' veins, flowers' hearts and the minutest curly thread-like blades of grass are drawn in with a very fine brush.

After adding the final touches, the artist put aside the tray which he had worked on with such skill, love and devotion and picked up another shiny black tray on which other flowers from the boundless garden of his imagination would spring to life. And in this manner his whole life was spent, day in, day out.

This craft, which emerged over a hundred and fifty years ago in primitive work-shops, is now being successfully developed at the modern Zhostovo decorative art factory whose handicraft articles are famous not only all over the Soviet Union but in many other countries besides. In the '30s large batches of Zhostovo trays with traditional floral designs were already being bought by France, England and the USA.

The Zhostovo artists' hand-painted trays were awarded medals at the New York World Exhibition in 1939 and at the Brussels World Exhibition in 1958. They have also won great acclaim at exhibitions in England, Czechoslovakia, Finland and Egypt.

And, of course, the Zhostovo trays are much sought after in Russia, too. Many are bought not only for practical purposes but also as decorations for walls and sideboards, and trays with blooming roses embellish thousands of homes. This traditional art is continuing to flourish in the Zhostovo artists' good hands.

"I Put up My Loom..."

"The snow's knee-deep, it's been snowing so hard today," Anna Sharonova informed me. Yes, I could see that for myself: the snowflakes were falling so thickly outside that I could barely make out the cottage opposite. I had been pursued by a snowstorm all the way to this formerly god-forsaken backwater in the Tver Gubernia, now the Kalinin Region. On the outskirts of Vesyegonsk the firs' shaggy branches were weighed down by heavy snow caps, and like ships with warm smoking funnels gliding through a boundless sea of snow, the wooden cottages dipped their bows into the white foaming snowdrifts.

Birch logs crackling in a stove, the tremendous heat coming from it, which always makes a town visitor's face glow, thick hundred-year-old timber walls with dry reddish moss in their grooves, which cut this cosy little world off from the biting and roaring blizzards, photographs of by-gone youth hanging on the walls – all these are touching relics of a happy and well-ordered way of life and prerogatives of a healthy peasant philosophy. And they all give you such a wonderful feeling of peace and calm.

> *I put up my loom,*
> *It's nine springs old,*
> *Nine springs old.*
> *Ten on Shrove Tuesday,*

sang Anna, accompanied by the lulling click of her loom on which she was weaving a never-ending rug. There were homespun rugs on the floors and walls all over the house, and thirty-metre runners tucked away in tight rolls on the cupboard tops, but Anna, who was used to working, could not let her loom stand idle or any scraps of material be wasted.

"This is my mother's loom. My husband's family, the Sharonovs, had one too but this one's smaller and neater, and I like it very much," she said, satisfying my curiosity for she had seen how I was admiring her wonderful loom with whose help until quite recently, less than two generations ago, Russian peasants had provided themselves with all the cloths and clothing they needed. "I don't know how old it is – it belonged to my great-grandmother and my mother's eighty-three, and, what's more, my great-grandmother's mother worked on it too.

"Now times have changed, of course. Nowadays young people buy and wear smart things whereas in the old days most of them had to wear homespun clothes. The wealthier folk could, of course, afford to buy them but we couldn't: there were

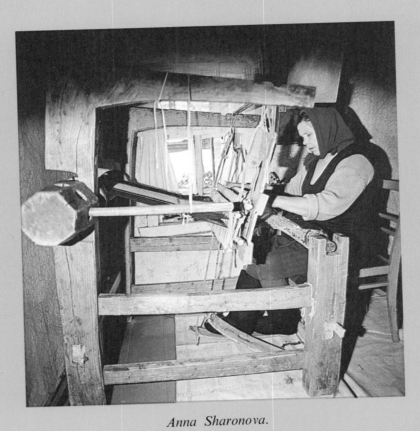

Anna Sharonova.

Anna Sharonova. Hand-woven runner. Fragment.

Weaver's house.

seven girls in our family and so at a very young age we all learnt to weave. Why, in Kreshnevo everyone used to weave – once the harvest was in, that's what we spent most of the time doing. And it wasn't just hard work, you know, it was a joy, too, to make such beautiful things with your own hands...

Anna kept a canvas bag full of remnants and balls of thread within easy reach and while we were talking, the shuttle slid to and fro, the loom clicked away as it picked up the new thread and the growing carpet turned on the shaft.

"Yes, the snow's knee-deep..." Anna sighed, glancing out of the frost-patterned window and we went on chatting.

Huzul Rugs

If I had not known I was in an ordinary house, I might well have thought I was in a rug museum for the walls of the rooms, the hall, stairs and verandah were all hung with Huzul rugs. There were *nizima* rugs embroidered with satin-stitch, pileless *kilims*, light-coloured fluffy woollen *djerga* but most of all, *kilims* of various colours and sizes, ranging from enormous wall-length ones to very small ones, the size of a serviette.

The house's owner and weaver of all these masterpieces, Gafia Vizichkanich gave me a guided tour of the rugs. "Each one is named either after its pattern –'Acorns', 'Daisies', 'Red Tulips' or after the mood which the weaver reckons it should evoke – 'Day-dreams', 'Spring'.

"You can always recognise a Huzul *kilim* straightaway," she continued, "because they're quite different to the rugs from elsewhere in the Ukraine. For a start, they always have wide transversal bands with complex patterns alternating with narrow, simpler ones. The main motif of the pattern consists mainly of large diamonds and hexagons with cogs, straight dashes and scrolls. And it's these different-coloured bands and very concise geometric pattern which cause the *kilim* to look so different from other rugs.

"But these are only its main features. Generally speaking, there are as many different *kilims* as there are villages. In each one they weave their own favourite pattern which is passed on from mother to daughter."

The design of each type of carpet is worked out precisely but only adhered to strictly at factories. At home, of course, they are free to improvise and the variations in the colour scheme give them practically unlimited potential for self-expression. Choosing various colours from the traditional light browns, yellows, reds and greens for the background and pattern, a weaver may create completely different carpets of the same design, either subtly coloured or very bright with sharply contrasting patterns and backgrounds. It is entirely a question of taste.

Going by the "exhibits" on show in her home, Gafia Vizichkanich preferred pure rich tones such as dark-red, deep green and mellow brown. The white diamonds, herring-bone and zigzags of the traditional Huzul motifs in which, as in all Huzul folk art, ancient symbols have been preserved, stand out against the backgrounds with remarkable clarity. The colour schemes, compositions and patterns themselves point to the weaver's impeccable artistic taste and technical expertise.

However, this is only to be expected for Gafia Vizichkanich, an honoured hand-

127

icraftswoman of the Ukrainian SSR, was long ago acclaimed one of the best rug-weavers in the Carpathian Mountains and awarded the Order of Lenin and other awards and prizes for her work.

...Gafia made her first rug at the age of fourteen. In the village of Ganychi where she was born (the ninth daughter in the family) and is still living, they used to weave everything for their homes – clothing, towels, table cloths, blankets, runners and mats. And though there were plenty of beautiful rugs around here, Gafia's was singled out at once, so beautifully fresh and consonant with Carpathian nature were

Gafia Vizichkanich. Embroidered kilim.

its colours. The talented girl was noticed by Pan Zagrada who was starting up a textile factory in the village at the time. The fine-fleeced wool spun by peasants, and talented work force cost him next to nothing while he was paid large sums of money in Europe for these homespun rainbow-coloured Huzul carpets. It was in his factory that Gafia wove her first rug. That was over fifty years ago. Then the factory owner started taking his talented weaver to exhibitions abroad where she would sit

Gafia Vizichkanich. Hand-woven kilim.

129

Gafia Vizichkanich.

Gafia Vizichkanich. Djerga.

at a loom all day, demonstrating her skills.

During the war the rug workshop was burned down by the Nazis but after the war they somehow managed to reconstruct four whole looms from separate details, and then Gafia asked the regional authorities for help. Soon a large construction project was set in motion in Ganychi and a new workshop with ten looms built in the village centre. The Huzul *kilim* was given a new lease of life. Of course, the workshop was run by Gafia and she also became its chief designer. All the rugs in her home are her original designs which are copied by the other weavers in the workshop. Although the folk traditions give much scope for fantasy, even they don't satisfy Gafia: all her life she has been looking for and finding in nature new colours, patterns and lines and transferring them to her rugs.

Gafia and I walked across the village to the workshop. How wonderfully fresh the air was in Ganychi! Abounding in greenery, the village lay in the wide valley of the Teresva between undulating tree-covered hills, and directly above the village the mountains clasped the river between stone palms, forming a picturesque canyon. The water was so crystal-clear that every pebble on the bottom sparkled in the sunlight. And there were flowers everywhere. It was therefore no wonder that there was so much life, harmony and colours in Huzul rugs.

A gentle breeze scented with grass and field flowers was playing round the large-windowed one-storey building of the rug workshop. Women were sitting on wooden benches on the grass outside the porch and winding wool into balls. Inside the workshop the atmosphere was just as cosy, homely and conducive to work. And judging by the women's expressions, smiles and cheerful jokes, they were in high spirits. The light flooded freely into the room through the large windows decorated with flowers. The looms stood in three rows with large gaps between. Gafia sat down and instantly picked up a well-known pattern for, as we have said, many of the rugs are woven to her designs. And after the shuttle had moved imperceptibly several times, a new weft was woven into the fabric.

Nearly all the young weavers in the workshop are Gafia's apprentices.

"Every year I take on three or maybe five apprentices," she told me, "and how long they study depends on their keenness and skill but, of course, not less than three months. And you need to work about three years to learn all the tricks of the trade. It's easier with a *kilim*: I make a little one and work everything out and then we make a big one from it. But it's harder with a *djerga* or *lizhnik*, as it's also called, which is woven out of thick, loosely-spun sheep's wool and then combed over and soaked in water for twenty-four hours, and not just in any old water but in a stream or whirlpool where the water will swirl round it and wash through the pile. In the old days it was soaked in the stream by the water-mill but now it's put in the rapids of the river, near the riverbank. During this procedure the carpet shrinks about half a metre but, to make up for it, becomes much thicker. A well processed and combed carpet of this sort is very fluffy and may be used to decorate your home, cover a bed or as a mountaineer's blanket."

As she spoke about the rugs, Gafia's lovely kind face lit up even more in a smile and I realised why she, now in the twilight of her life, was making *kilims* with names like, "Maiden's Plait", "Day-dreams", and "Spring"...

Who Can Make a Nightingale Sing?

Everyone has his very own star in the sky. So thought many in Sheki, including old Rza Tagi Zade.

Sheki lies high up in the Caucasus Mountains. The air here is transparent and the star-studded sky very close. It seems that if you were to go up to the highest mountain at night, you could reach up to one.

He did, however, believe that he had found his star and that every time he picked up his tambour, known locally as *sakhna*, stretched a piece of velvet across it, picked up his fine steel crochet (*garmag*) and began embroidering a new pattern in silk thread, his sacred star lit up the room. *Tekelduz*, the ancient name in Azerbaijan for the craft of embroidering velvet or fine woollen cloth in silk thread on a tambour, was translated as "one star" by the embroiderers who still practised this craft which is so highly revered by Sheki menfolk.

This craft came into being long ago. In the 16th and 17th centuries high-quality Azerbaijan silk was already a chief export to Russia, Iran, Turkey, India, Italy and other countries. And by then embroidery was already one of the most popular and common forms of folk art. For example, in an Azerbaijan poem *Leili and Medjnun* by Fizuli, Leili's mother advises her to take up the noblest art form – embroidery. The wide development of various types of embroidery in sixteenth-century Azerbaijan was also noted by many other poets, historians and foreign travellers. For instance, Englishmen describing the surroundings in which the Shirvan-Shahs lived, wrote, "The king was sitting in a lavish marquee embroidered with silk and gold." "Their main occupation is spinning, weaving and embroidering in silk and cotton... In the vaulted niches there were various scarfs woven in brightly-coloured silk and gold," wrote Adam Olearius, a Schleswig-Holstein diplomat in Russia, in the 17th century after visiting various towns in Azerbaijan. From other sources we learn of the special embroidery workshops which existed at the time. The most popular forms of embroidery were tambour *tekelduz*, *giulyabetin* (golden-threaded embroidery), *mundjuklu* (beaded embroidery) and *gurama* (appliqué), and the acknowledged centre of *tekelduz* embroidery was Sheki.

Not long ago at all, it seems, this ancient art form was still being continued here by the masters Abas Aga-Agayev, Mamed Ali, Ali-Abas-Tagiev and Salman Navrug-ogly but in Sheki time rushes by as swiftly as a mountain river, and imperceptibly the day came when in Sheki and all Azerbaijan, only *usto* Rza, as acclaimed masters are called here, could call to life on his tambour dazzlingly bright peacocks

133

Mokhtaram Agagusinzade with a pupil.

Decorative embroidery. Sheki. 19th century.

and trilling nightingales (*biul-biuls*), and cause the roses and daffodils on his embroidered cushions to smell sweetly. But then he died, too, and on his death bed he bequeathed his tambour to his daughter whom he had taught to embroider as a little girl, and in this way the art, which had flourished in Sheki for four centuries, was passed into the hands of Mokhtaram.

When her father died, a bright star fell from the sky and extinguished over the mountains, and Mokhtaram started searching for her own star to make her home and life brighter...

Mokhtaram Agagusinzade. Embroidered cushion-cover.

Up and down, up and down quickly ran the crochet and a short white stitch was left on the black cloth. And these stitches grew into a gently curving line in which I caught the outline of a petal. When the entire surface had been patterned with white thread, it had to be filled in the same manner with dense rows of bright coloured silk. Mokhtaram held the tambour on her lap with her left hand and embroidered with her right. You could not see the thread on the right side as the crochet picked it up on the reverse side and pulled it through the velvet. A perfectly even line was formed without any preliminary pattern. The flowery design along the edges was

136

ready and she was now embroidering the central pattern.

Although it looked incredibly simple, it took years of hard work to get the lines to run so smoothly and surely, and only the most skilled needlewomen were capable of achieving such a wonderfully symmetrical pattern and superb and sensitive gamut of colour.

A true artist always has pupils and so too does Mokhtaram. Shakla, Arzu, Sevil and two Mokhabats, all fifth-formers, are sitting beside her at the table, sewing wobbly stitches. A school embroidery class is in process. The girls' tambours are three times smaller than their teacher's. Embroidering beautiful cushion-covers, bedspreads, bath mats and many other household items is long and laborious work. Mokhtaram embroiders in all her free time after work.

"I like embroidering very much and would happily do nothing else, but *tekelduz* is now a museum art and all my embroideries go to museums or exhibitions. Of course, I'm very glad to have my works displayed next to those of my father and the other old embroiderers but it would be nicer to make them for people to use. It's quite feasible to revive the old tradition. My daughters, for instance, are very keen on embroidery for, you see, it's wonderful to be able to make people's lives more beautiful! In the last century there used to be special embroidery workshops in Sheki which were famous far and wide. They could be set up again now for Sheki is still the centre of the silk industry just as it always was. My girls would be happy to work there."

...The embroidery class is over for the day. The pupils put their needlework into bags. Let's hope they too will catch their lucky star in the wonderful art of *tekelduz*.

Dawn was just breaking over the Daghestan mountain village of Kubachi when white spots began moving here and there on its dark steep slopes as the womenfolk and young girls set out to fetch water from the spring in their traditional knee-length white shawls (*kaz*). Each was carrying on her back a tall and large but elegant and slender ten-litre copper vessel (*muchal*), and tied to it in front was an equally shiny but twice as small jug (*kutka*), both chased articles, unique in shape and design. The Kubachi womenfolk's snow-white and gold-embroidered shawls are also beautiful. And so is the Caucasian village itself, famous for its gunsmiths and goldsmiths. Having totally retained its colourful and unique way of life, it is an exotic medieval town with endless labyrinthine lanes which are dark even in broad daylight, narrow steps carved out of the rocks, blind alleys and donkeys clicking along its polished stony streets. Ancient stones with carvings of monsters taken from old dilapidated buildings, peer from the houses' grey walls and a goat's skull presides over the peace. A mighty round stone buttress tower crowns the pyramid of houses with flat roofs on which the villagers spend half their lives, and thanks to the special acoustics, chat away to their neighbours without the help of telephones. You won't find a single woman here who walks about without her needlework of some kind. For instance, they knit wonderful thick socks called *djuraba* from coloured wool. On the platform (*gudekan*) made of raised stone slabs and carved pillars you will see sedate old men in tall dark-brown astrakhan hats holding onto heavy canes who look just as much like stone sculptures as the ancient pillars. Here, on the platform, young people learn the history and legends of Kubachi from the old men, discoursing in a slow and pensive manner. They hear, too, of the old craftsmen's ancient customs, and with the tip of a cane a dark wrinkled hand will firmly trace on the ground the outlines of a familiar design.

The sun had at last reached the mountains' crest and the early morning haze had gradually cleared, opening up even farther vistas of the mountainous countryside, the silvery winding river far below and the snowy peaks. Down below the alpine meadows were still not in full bloom and only a few sheep were lazily cropping the grass – the flocks would be driven here a little later.

Gleaming on the hazy horizon was a narrow bluish-grey streak of sea. It was probably about forty kilometres to the Caspian in a straight line but the road there, consisting of a series of hairpin bends across rocky terrain, took about two hours, if not three, to cover. In the spring and summer you could hardly ever see the sea from the village platform as this was one of the special favours granted by clear cool autumn days. So, this was considered a good sign.

From this bird's eye view of the distant deep-blue Caspian Sea you understood why a thousand years ago the Arabian traveller, Al-Masudi, had written that the fabulous country of Urbug was too inaccessible to be attacked by neighbouring tribes. Be that as it may, very near Kubachi, which was built like an eagle's nest on a sharp-pointed cliff, wars and clashes never ceased for many centuries. The narrow strip of flat land between the Caspian and the eastern spurs of the Caucasus, which linked the Nogai Steppe in the north with Persia in the south, was used as a pass by the hordes of nomads, Persians, Arabs and Turks. Waves of invaders got as far as the village, too. Among the many legends here, one goes as follows: when the village was besieged by Turkish troops, the villagers poured quicklime into water-bearing copper vessels, put them out on the roof-tops and at dawn started slaking it with water. And the Turks, reckoning it was smoke from cannon fuses, beat a hasty retreat.

For centuries villages were named after their inhabitants' craft. Kubachi—armourers—was so named by the Turks in the 16th century. Previously, this region had been known as the land of *Zirekhgerans*—cuirassiers and armourers. Two thousand years ago the territory of present-day Kubachi formed part of Caucasian Albania, the only vestiges of which are to be seen in the form of "Albanian" copper cauldrons and in the designs on the stone tombstones which local goldsmiths consider prototypes of their art.

In those far-off days, according to the Greek geographer Strabo, the local people "worshipped the Sun, Zeus and the Moon". Conquerors came and went, and so did religions—first paganism, and then Christianity and Islam. Everything, in fact, changed, except the villagers' trade. As early as the 12th century the Arabian historian Abu Hamid Andalusi wrote, "The *Zirekhgerans* make all sorts of weapons, chain mail, helmets, swords, bows, daggers' sheaths and various copper wares. They have neither arable lands nor orchards but they're a prosperous people and they are brought all manner of things from various parts."

It was, of course, not the lands where the almond trees only blossomed on the rocky crags when the walnut trees were already bearing fruit on the coast that attracted the foreign commanders, princes, shahs, emirs and sultans but the fame of this highly prosperous town abounding in skilled jewellers and gunsmiths who had supplied the whole of the Caucasus with armour. "Our grandfathers paid Shah Nadir off with one sabre," the old men recalled, "and Shamil * himself sent his men to fetch an expensive weapon, and Khadji-Murat, another great man of these mountains, came in person to order a dagger." Weapons from here were taken far afield. In the Moscow Kremlin's Armoury, for instance, there is a sabre belonging

---

* Shamil (1799-1871)—the commander of the Caucasian people's war of liberation against colonialists and local feudal lords.—*Ed.*

to Prince Mstislavsky which was made by Kubachi craftsmen in the 16th century. Very fine double chain mail which provided excellent protection from sabre and dagger blows as well as arrows, and costly cuirasses for great commanders were made in Kubachi, and in the neighbouring village of Amuzghi genuine damask steel was made which the Kubachi smiths mounted in silver, gold and ivory.

The sun was rising higher and higher over the village, warming its stones. Among the villagers to gather on the square's time-worn stones was Rasul Alikhanov, a highly esteemed hereditary craftsman, People's Artist of the Russian Federation

Kubachi. Medieval carved stone on the wall of a house.

and Ilya Repin State Prize winner. He likes coming here when he has finished work on a silver water ewer, *kumgan*, dish or dagger, to rest for a while after many days' work and chat with the other craftsmen about his beloved craft and his problems connected with it, and inhale Kubachi's bracing air. Despite his sixty-odd years, over fifty of which he has devoted to art, Rasul is a youthful and energetic man with an animated expression.

It is greatly to Rasul Alikhanov's credit that Kubachi villagers are zealously preserving the old traditions of the best Caucasian jewellers as he has been teaching this ancestral art to young people for many years and has brought all his eight sons up as artists. At eight Rasul was already helping his own grandfather, Akhmed, in the smithy.

He learnt the art of making jewellery from his father, Alikhan Akhmedov, a highly-skilled specialist in the minutest designs who engraved and chased sabre and dagger handles, belts, buckles, cigarette cases. And Alikhan had studied under his uncle, Ishim Usayev, who was considered the village's best craftsman at the end of the last century. Rasul's father used to tell him stories about his stern teacher look-

Kubachi. By the water-spring.

ing captiously over the top of his glasses at his pupils' articles, and if he noticed the slightest imperfection, he would mercilessly crush the finished article with a hammer and set a new task. If, however, he was pleased with the work, Ishim who was stingy with his praise, would merely comment that it was a "vivid design".

In Kubachi, which looms over the ravine like a multi-tiered amphitheatre, every house seems to be growing out of the roof of the one below and the flat roofs, the only horizontal surfaces, are used by people as small open courtyards where they spend a considerable part of their daily lives. It was here that I was taken by Rasul

141

to continue our conversation about Kubachi art and artists. This, however, did not prevent him from picking up an instrument and continuing work with his son, Ibragim. What's more, each was doing something different: Rasul was working on a large dish and his son on a bracelet.

During his fifty years as a jeweller Rasul has constantly studied the artistic heritage of preceeding generations of craftsmen and meditated upon the craft's past, present and future. He has copied on paper patterns of practically all the old Kubachi articles such as ornaments on old stone walls and pictorial carvings on stones from destroyed 14th-16th century houses which have been set in the walls of houses. He has interpreted all this material and his own experience in a definitive piece of research entitled *The Art of Kubachi* which was published in Moscow in 1971.

Great credit is due to Rasul Alikhanov for also developing Kubachi art. Besides being most ardently in favour of carefully preserving all Kubachi's ancient traditions and artistic originality, he is also an innovator for while using old types of ornaments or jewellery techniques, a true skilled craftsman always contributes something of his own creative individuality. And Rasul is no exception. It is namely he who has introduced to Kubachi chasing the motif of flowers. It is not for nothing that among the pencils, chisels and cutters on his work table you will find field flowers, dried leaves and stems. And after many centuries he was the first to dare to reintroduce into traditional decorations images of wild beasts and animals such as snow leopards, wolves, deer and horses which were forbidden by the Koran. With equal daring he has refuted the less restrained types of patterns – *marharai*, "bushes", "branches" in favour of a freer pattern, paying more attention to the character and form of the material itself and shape of the article, which was characteristic of the early Kubachi works, especially of women's jewellery of the 17th and 18th centuries.

The older the jewellery, the more sculptured the form and more resplendent the colour scheme. A significant role was played by the smithing and casting; coloured stones were mounted in highly-raised, prominent massive settings, and the large and small gold or silver balls and filigree all around also greatly added to the beautiful shape of the bracelet, brooch, ring or pendant. In later articles made at the end of the 18th, and in the 19th century the decorative style of the surface gained increasingly more significance, as did the filigree, niello and small-scale engraving and chasing, inlaying and intricate design at which Kubachi jewellers excelled.

You can easily tell the difference between old and later articles of jewellery when the Kubachi womenfolk come out to celebrate the traditional spring festival "Forty Days of Spring" in May which has served as an original bride-show for many centuries here. All the jewellery, which has been preserved in each family, is worn at this festival, and there are enough pendants, earrings, necklaces, bracelets and rings to fill a large museum. Numerous examples of all the various methods of artistically treating metal are on display here – smithing, forging, engraving, chasing, niello, damascening and filigree. The massive silver articles are lavishly encrusted with cornelians, corals, almandines, turquoises, garnets, jasper, lapis lazuli and coloured glass. On some articles you can see motifs of birds, snakes and horses, ancient symbols which may be traced back to pagan times when such items were used as amulets.

Alikhanov's main idea and goal is to reinstate the old traditional methods of making jewellery and decorative pieces of art, which time out of mind have played a highly significant part in Daghestan mountain people's lives, especially in Kubachi where practically every man was a goldsmith.

"Here in Kubachi we love and value our art," he said, "for you see, it has been our whole life for many centuries. And today our menfolk still work with silver and copper and our women still weave, knit and embroider. You could hardly find as many artists in a large town as we have here in our village. And like all artists, we're constantly searching for new ideas and closely studying the articles of other craftsmen.

"The end of the 19th and beginning of the 20th century marked a special period in the history of our village. Some craftsmen in dire straits went off to other towns in the Northern Caucasus and further afield while others set off to Moscow, St. Petersburg, the capitals of Europe and even America in search of fame and glory. While winning wide acclaim, our art drifted away from its original sources. The world regarded us, first and foremost, as craftsmen equally skilled at all the various jewellery techniques. Sophisticated articles with excessively lavish designs were demanded of us and so we made them, knowing full well, however, that our real art had always been much more austere, profound and noble. And this contradiction has always troubled us. In my most important works I have always tried to reintroduce various of these lost traditions. It was for this reason that I studied the particular features of our designs and copied them not only in my jewellery articles but also in wood, stone and ivory carvings and embroidery. The result of this work has been that many of our craftsmen's designs have become purer, more expressive and closer to its original sources.

"Then Hadji-Bakhmud Magomedov and some other craftsmen started using the traditional local themes on stone carvings and reliefs on forged bronze cauldrons to decorate our articles. For instance, from these reliefs we took motifs of mythical wild animals; we also started using the traditional shapes of unique Kubachi brass and copper embossed articles such as *muchala, kunne,* and *kutka.* And as for jewellery, well, I reckon they should once again become an important part of Kubachi art. I have to admit that namely in this area, strange as it may seem, we are still very cautious about using traditional art forms. Perhaps it's because we're afraid that the unusual shapes of our old bracelets, rings, and belts will not be to buyers' tastes or perhaps we've simply forgotten some of the devices used by our ancestors. But I'm still certain we should reinstate these traditions which are so important as far as the techniques of Kubachi art are concerned for the most important task in our creative work is namely to keep our originality. We and our children need the experience of our fathers and grandfathers whose memory we revere, just as we need the invigorating fresh air of Kubachi, the best place in the whole wide world."

Of course, Rasul is right: it is essential to look after traditions, especially in such a unique village as Kubachi where the true beauty of an article, its pattern and design are very acutely felt and where there is a veritable cult of old art. In the guest room of nearly every house you will find the most varied old objects of art – rugs, arms, china, and decorative pieces from China, India, Persia, Egypt and Turkey, which were brought to the village by the craftsmen who did seasonal work in the

From Rasul Alikhanov's family collection.

south of Russia, Near East and Central Asia but mostly you will see items made by local masters.

Rasul Alikhanov showed me his remarkable collection which had been put together by many generations of craftsmen. There were quite a few bronze, copper and brass items with traditional repoussé engraved designs exemplifying the degree of perfection attained by Kubachi craftsmen for whom each household item was elevated to the level of a work of art. The exhibition was arranged in a strictly systematic order, with the solid and more simply decorated cauldrons with relief pat-

Rasul Alikhanov and his son, Ibragim.

terns below a shelf of conical waterbearing vessels (*muchala*) with cylindrical lids and wide bottoms covered with traditional chased scalloped patterns and decorative riveting in joining the separate pieces of the vessel. The next row above was occupied by repoussé brass vessels (*nuknus*) similar to wide-bottomed buckets. Next came the vessels known as *kutka*, jugs, *kumgans*, dishes and other crockery. Traditionally an essential part of a mountain girl's dowry, the copper vessels, were always polished until they shone for in these mountains it was generally believed that the shine drove evil spirits out of the house. The next wall was covered all over

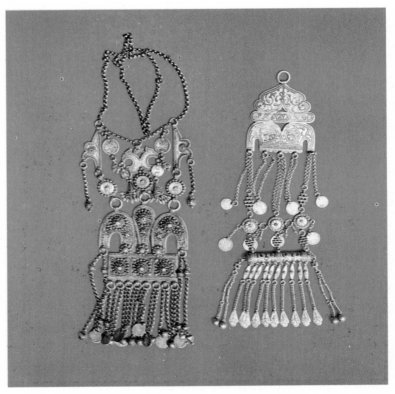

Articles by 19th-century
Kubachi jewellers.

with china and glazed earthenware dishes alongside superb women's jewellery of the 18th and 19th centuries, open-work belts, buckles, pendants, earrings, and, of course, daggers.

"I've always been mad about daggers," Rasul admitted, "you see, according to an old legend, the first Kubachi villager's baby was born with a dagger in one hand and a jeweller's graver in the other. I couldn't tell you how many different blades, old and new, I've mounted on handles and as soon as I've made one, I'm already

146

thinking about the next. And now I've decided to put all my expertise into making a new dagger, and I've already ordered a blade from Kurban Rabatov, the last Amuzghi smith, who knows how to make damask steel."

...Amuzghi is an old semi-abandoned village about three kilometres away. To get there you have to go along a winding mountain track which offers quite a few more impressions to the bewitched traveller by bringing together in an amazing manner the unreal beauty of the Caucasian foothills and wonderful real medieval scenery. On the right, for instance, is an old carved tombstone belonging to a sheikh who

Kubachi daggers: an antique dagger in the centre,
works by Rasul Alikhanov on either side.

lived long ago. It is sheltered by a canopy of acacia branches festooned with dozens of different-coloured sun-bleached rags and scraps of paper – an old way of decorating particularly hallowed places. And already looming ahead are the ruins of the village of Amuzghi where at one time famous damask steel, the best in all the Caucasus, was forged in as many as fifty smithies. At first, everything here seemed to be lying at eternal rest. Then as I climbed up the narrow crooked lanes of the ruined citadel, I noticed obvious signs of life – a roaming donkey, pots and pans outside.

Wonders, it seemed, would never cease, and I wouldn't have been at all surprised if Ali-Baba or Alladin had come sauntering out from behind the mounds of yellow sandstone. And then among the ruins there really did appear two little figures, young inhabitants of a village which had been almost totally abandoned, who guided me to a smithy with a blazing furnace.

A grey-bearded man in a sheepskin hat was forging an elegant narrow-tipped blade. It appeared that Kurban Rabatov, the last of the renowned Amuzghi gun-smiths, now made daggers for song and dance companies. "No, these aren't the same as the damask steel blades which used to be forged from three strips of differ-ent kinds of steel – soft and pliant *dugalala* for the solid part, strong *antushka* for the blade and the strongest sort, *alkhana*, for the hilt," explained the old man sadly, "you see, this sort of steel isn't needed for souvenir daggers." A sorrowful and rather embarrassed expression came into the eyes of the last custodian of the secrets of damask steel which had once brought the villagers of Amuzghi such great fame because he, Kurban Rabatov, was making a fake weapon, unworthy of his mastery, and of his wrinkled hands which had become tanned from working with hot metal.

"I'm making my last damask steel blade for Rasul Alikhanov," said the old man, his eyes lighting up again, "may it always remind my friend of Amuzghi craftsmen."

On my way back from Amuzghi past a bend in the stony path I suddenly caught sight of Kubachi from a new angle, and at once recalled one of Alikhanov's chased plates with a view of the village. The Kubachi people's proud and secluded world had obviously been depicted from this spot in the shape of a pyramid of houses, huddled closely together. "Kubachi men only marry Kubachi girls and our girls only marry Kubachi men," Rasul had told me. "Why? It's all very simple: firstly, because you won't in the world find a better wife and, secondly, because even inhabitants from neighbouring villages can't understand our language."

Yes, such is this amazing village whose infertile stony soil has forced its hard-working people into becoming consummate craftsmen. A world of its own for thousands of years, it has acquired its own tenor of life, too. Hidden away from bel-licose and menacing neighbours on a rock cliff-top, Kubachi villagers have kept their secrets of making arms and gold articles as a pledge of their independence and very existence.

Both Clothing and Bedding

Though small in area and dissected by deep ravines, mountainous Daghestan simply abounds in the most varied arts and crafts, such as wood carvings, incrustations and carpets to name but a few. Whichever way you go from Kubachi, you're absolutely bound to come across another village of wonderful craftsmen and old traditions.

In Daghestan, people who live in or come from the Avar village of Andi are considered lucky because whatever they lay their hands on, turns out marvellously. And it's really true. Take, for example, my archeologist friend, Khizri Amirkhanov. Three years ago he started excavating a ruin whose identity had supposedly been established long ago, near the mountain village of Chokh and determined that it was a very old, unique settlement, giving grounds to affirm that the Caucasus was one of the world's main independent centres of early agriculture! And how did it all start? When a local miller came up to the archeologists' campfire when they were digging nearby, and started lighting his pipe with a flint which the scientists found highly interesting. The miller then showed them the spot where he had found it, and they made a trial excavation which immediately revealed a deep untouched cultural stratum. Yes, you have to admit, Andi villagers certainly are lucky!

It is also said that whenever you hear a particularly funny joke or story, you're bound to find an Andi villager nearby. And that's true, too. According to an old custom, when a son is born in Andi, his delighted father fires his shotgun to let the whole district know. Apparently, one day while an Andi villager was staying at his friend's home in a neighbouring district, a son was born to the family, and, much to everyone's surprise, the Andi man suddenly started firing his shotgun. "What are you shooting for – it's not your son who's born?" the puzzled villagers asked him reasonably. "I'm happy a new farmhand's been born," replied the latter with a smile. You see, the people of Andi are also famous for their sheep but they don't like mowing hay and prefer to hire farmhands from neighbouring villages instead. They are also famous for their superb felt cloaks (*burka*) made from sheep's wool. After passing the regional centre, Botlikh, we drove through the Andi region with the fast-flowing gurgling river on our left, and headed for the village of Rakhata, famous for its *burka* industry.

Until recently a mountain inhabitant's most essential equipment were a dagger and felt cloak. The felt cloak is practical clothing for it is totally impervious to the

Daghestan – a land of mountains.

wind and rain and serves a traveller or shepherd as a bed. You can lie down on the damp ground in any weather, cover yourself with it and just forget about everything. And you can roll it up tightly and hitch it to your belt or saddle. It will protect you from the frost, rain and sabre blows.

Just as the best arms in the Caucasus have been made in Kubachi for the past thousand years, so the best felt cloaks have been made in the Daghestan village of Andi. There is a tremendous demand for them in Georgia, Armenia, Azerbaijan and on the River Don not only because Andi craftsmen are more skilled than others but also because a special breed of sheep with excellent wool has been bred here in Andi.

Whereas nowadays you only see a Circassian coat and dagger on the odd villager at a festival or on a stage artiste, you see people in felt cloaks going about their everyday work. True, they make very few of them now in Andi and only for their own needs or for close relatives and friends but in the nearby village of Rakhata a small factory has been in operation since 1924, making felt cloaks in the traditional method.

Washing felt.

The river pointed the way to the village: a black streak suddenly appeared in its clear fast-flowing waters and led us all the way to the bridge under which a man in high rubber boots was trampling black felt underfoot in a small creek shut off by stones. The sinister-looking effluent flowing out of the creek caused us to query the ecological efficacy of such a method of washing felt but we tactfully said nothing and got acquainted with the man washing the felt, Magomed Abdulgadjiev. A few minutes later when he had rinsed all the felt cloaks and thrown them dripping-wet onto two mules, we all set off in this picturesque company towards the factory

151

Preparing felt for a white burka.

which turned out to be very small and only about a hundred metres from the bridge.

Apparently, the felt cloaks took a whole week to make, that is, just as long as many centuries ago, and although we were unable to follow the whole process from start to finish, we still managed to see separate stages of it.

There did not seem to be anything particularly complicated about it. The crafts-women laid a layer of wool, a few centimetres thick, in the shape of a felt cloak on a special rug and then made it into a big roll and started pounding it all over with their

Horseman in a burka.

elbows. This had to be done evenly and for quite some time to ensure that the wool was beaten down into a tight even layer, the same thickness all over. Then the roller was opened and the material dyed black (only a few expensive white felt cloaks are made for special clients and gifts).

After the dyed felt cloaks had been combed with a special tool and the wool fluffed up, came the most important stage when all the motes were taken off the wool and flax-foot besoms were run over the felt until its hairs twisted into tiny plaits which made the cloak impervious. Then it was washed in the river in the man-

153

ner we had already seen.

Picking up one of the dried cloaks by its edges, the craftswomen stretched it out in the air like a blanket and started carefully dipping the lower part into a sticky solution in a large iron tub. Now the little plaits stuck together and provided reliable protection against bad weather for many years to come. All that was left now was to sew the cloak together with strong thread and give it the traditional cut of a loose cape with pointed shoulders. An ordinary cloak costs between seventy to ninety roubles and so anyone can afford one. They get orders even from Central Asia. "Our felt cloaks are worn by Rasul Gamzatov *, astronauts and Fidel Castro," the factory workers told me with legitimate pride.

As I really wanted to take a picture of an Andi horseman wearing a felt cloak in the place of origin of this fine mountain clothing, I started looking round in the hope of spotting one and he was soon to appear. Sitting agilely in the saddle, his head high, he rode slowly straight through the factory gates, playing indolently with his whip. When I asked permission to photograph him, he consented condescendingly and was at once fetched an excellent cloak, the colour of a raven's wing, which had just been finished.

And when he flung it on, he looked just like an eagle soaring over the mountains. The sun had already vanished behind the ridge and I had only a few minutes to take the picture. The horseman with the chiselled profile was splendid and fairly patient to boot but when I started changing the film, he snapped, "Look, I've been standing here in the wind for ten minutes and I'm frozen stiff."

"You're right," I replied, "you really might catch cold but, you see, I'm photographing you for a book and not for a family album and I'll have to write that the people of Andi gave Fidel Castro a gift of a felt cloak which one might get frozen stiff in on a warm August evening."

The horseman smiled, flashing a gold tooth. He must have realised that the Andi people's good humour, which, evidently, even the local terrain exuded, was also transmitted to any newcomer who grew genuinely fond of this region.

---

* A renowned contemporary Daghestan poet.– Ed.

In the valleys spring had already come into its own. During the day the sun was nearly as hot as in summer, leaving the retreating winter a chance to make itself felt only during the chilly nights. But with the first rays of the sun, the earth, waiting to be sown, grew warmer and so did the air, too, and the orchards seemed to burst into flower simultaneously, filling the air with the sweet fragrance of almonds, apricots, apples and cherries. There was a joyful feeling of renewal in nature, which was felt by people also.

It is not without reason that time out of mind spring has been considered the morning of the year. Just as dawn brings the bright sun out of the dark deserts of the night, so spring leads it out from behind the winter mists. In Central Asia and Iran the New Year festivities *Navruz Bairam* celebrated on the day of the vernal Equinox, March 21, literally mean "new day".

Spring has also come to the Tadzhik village of Safedob ("Clear Water") in the Kulyab region, which in the '50s moved down from the spurs of the Pamir Mountains to the valley and future cotton fields. Sharifa Safarova, one of the region's best craftswomen, brought her old spinning wheel, which she had inherited from her grandmother and mother, and an equally old wooden loom to the new village. She always weaves and then embroiders with her daughter, Zebi, extremely beautiful *suzani*, large wall-length rectangular panels on a cotton or silk backcloth for the festivities.

"When you embroider *suzani*," she told me, "it's very important to choose the right technique for embroidering each pattern and seam and, of course, the right colour for the threads. Large surfaces are best filled with one-sided satin stitch which produces a smooth, slightly relief pattern or *yurma*, a small stitch, creating a play of shades. This stitch is also used for edging and outlining the pattern. But if you really want to find out about the art of *suzani*, you'd better go to the mountains because that's where it originally came from, as did the pictures on the *suzani* of the sun, which is much closer in the mountains, and of tulips in the mountain valleys."

...And so here I was in Sharifa's, and the fine old craft's birthplace. Once free of snow, the Pamir foothills were soon covered with fresh green grass which advanced on the snow-white mountain caps above. While snowdrops were still flowering on the northern slopes, crimson tulips, poppies and roemerias were already blossoming on the southern ones. After hanging on the trees all winter, the pistachios were bitter-tasting. A mountain partridge bobbing on a branch covered with delicate

Weavers of the village of Iol.

leaves grew agitated. It was now too hot for the stone partridges in the village of Iol on the banks of the turbulent fast-flowing River Pyandzh and they were drawn higher towards the glaciers glinting icily among the clouds.

For six months of the year the village of Iol is cut off from the rest of the world by an impassable snowy pass and you can only get here in a light aircraft from the regional centre – if you're lucky, that is, for during the flight you have to make a series of complicated zigzags over the mountain ravines, hugging very close to the rocks and the whole way the sky has to be clear of the dense billowing clouds which usually linger here for a long time. So it's not hard to understand why the coming *Navruz Bairam* means much more to the villagers of Iol than it does to people down in the valleys. It heralds the forthcoming opening of the pass and way into the world and links with relatives and friends.

The mountains once gave people refuge for the first time, and here they learned to graze cattle and sow grain. And these most ancient hearths of civilization tend to preserve an archaic way of life, morals, manners, customs and folk art much more zealously than valleys. Now the people of Iol, famous for its ancient traditions, are

Suzani.

getting ready for the New Year festivities very carefully, trying not to omit any minute detail from the many diverse celebrations.

So far you cannot actually see these preparations, and all is peaceful and quiet in the village except for the occasional piercing brays of a mule. They are, however, in full swing for what would the festivities be like without a beautiful new *suzani*?

The word *suzani* or *siuzané*, as it is pronounced in Tadzhik and Uzbek respectively, has a certain indefinable charm. Joyful, light and ethereal like poplar fluff, it seems to have been invented by poets and dreamers. There's something esoteric and

Sharifa Safarova.

mysterious about it. It captures your imagination every time you go inside a Tadzhik's house because you know that as soon as you step out of the blazing hot yard flooded with unbearably bright sunlight into the cool, you will at once see staring at you from the wall the two huge enigmatic eyes of a sun, the *suzani*'s set pattern, shining nearly as brightly as the real one outside. And it is framed by dozens of slightly smaller white, golden and crimson suns, a vague allusion to the mountain people's most ancient notions of outer space, and the origin, creation and evolution of the universe. You stand and gaze in wonder at the pattern for a long time, which,

Suzani *in a festive glade.*

despite being almost invariably the same subject, is always so boundlessly diverse.

Local craftswomen have long since vyed with each other to embroider the most beautiful *suzani* for the New Year festivities. They are hung out for a public review and then the clay walls shine with all the colours of the rainbow. And the best is given the honour of decorating the festive glade or, to be more precise, green mountain slope where the *darkhastan*, festive table, is set and where a feast, with music, dancing and singing takes place. It is suspended on two long poles and even on a dull day the two huge pagan suns blaze over the revelries.

159

"If you want to look at the most beautiful *suzani*, go and see Shamigul Tago-rova," the villagers told me. And, indeed, hanging in her house were *suzani* whose patterns seemed to have been embroidered by the sun's rays themselves. She was sitting and working with her daughter, Begima, and daughter-in-law, Sairambi, on a large patterned felt sheet in her small yard. They were finishing off a long piece of work and had only the edges left to hem. Her *suzani* was certainly worthy of the *Navruz* which the whole village was eagerly awaiting.

And so at last came the long-awaited day, *Navruz Bairam*, New Year, extolled by many great poets of antiquity. The older children were the first to hurry to the festivities and by noon the large green slope was ablaze with colourful costumes. And in the highest spot for all to see hung the most beautiful *suzani* and, of course, it was the one I had seen at Shamigul's. The musicians had settled in its shade and the sounds of their national instruments rippled over the valley. Songs were sung and then dancers slowly formed a small circle in front of the orchestra and started moving smoothly and gracefully. But when the musicians played faster, they began flashing by and all the striped padded coats, brightly-coloured dresses and scarves blended into a bright speck of light...

Revival

Fabulous Birds

It had been worth coming to Voloshka just to see Petukhov's house. A beautiful wooden house with carved platbands and an ornament on the peak of its gable is no rarity here in the Russian North but whereas all the other old houses' woodwork had been blackened by time and bad weather, this house's pinewood was covered with light, shiny oil, and there were lavish wood carvings all over its porch, and window frames, and all the way up its log sides. And the house itself was long with a section for livestock and poultry: a real peasant's house of the sort no longer built in this village of wood-cutters. It testified not only to its owner's skills as a builder but to his unusual personality.

After pacifying a large ginger dog which was rushing at me and barking ferociously, a tall middle-aged man with a penetrating stare came out to meet me.

He put the samovar on and settled me down to warm up after my journey and started telling me his story. "I was born", he said, "in Malaya Shalga, near Kargopol, about fifty kilometres away from here, as the crow flies. There were six villages in Malaya Shalga. All the menfolk went in for farming during the summer and handicrafts in the winter and summer before fairs. They used to make baskets, tubs, barrels and casks and sell them at Kargopol market or take them to fairs in other towns like Arkhangelsk, Shenkursk, Vytegra, Oshevensk, Onega and even St. Petersburg. So they knew all about handicrafts but they didn't use to sell art objects much because they mostly made them for themselves. We, of course, decorated our houses with wood carvings because, you see, it's nicer living in a beautiful house.

"I fell in love with beautiful things as a young lad. I couldn't go past a beautiful house without stopping to stare. In my childhood, at the end of the '20s and beginning of the '30s, there were hardly any toys on sale except for clay whistles at the market and so either the father or grandfather used to make them for his children. As long as I can remember, I used to make wooden toys myself and decorate them with carvings. By the time I was eight, I was already carving wood quite well: I had a special sort of memory – I only had to see something once and I'd remember it forever. Later on this skill of mine as a child stood me in good stead. The collective farms needed sledges and sleighs and father used to make them in the evenings and I'd help him. We never went in for handicrafts – we didn't have the time but when I moved to Voloshka, and started building myself a house, I decided to decorate it like they did in the old days. The only tools I had were a plane, an axe and a hunting knife but as I worked, I made myself new tools. Then, as luck would have it, I decided to make some wooden birds to go in my house just as they had in the old days, too.

"And, you know, my surname is Petukhov * and my family can be traced back to Kulikovo Battle in the 14th century. One of my distant ancestors served as a commanding officer's batman and one of his duties was to wake up the troops during campaigns in the morning. You see, they didn't have alarm clocks in those days and so along with the spear, which he hunted bears and went into battle with, he also

Alexander Petukhov's house.

carried a cockerel in the sack on his back and it was by cockerels that they were ordered to get up and go to bed so that's just what they did. He came back to the village with this cockerel and his nickname stuck. And when they started registering all the peasants, they put him down as Petukhov from the village of Danilovka. But do you know how our Earth and all the Universe came about?" he asked, suddenly

---

* *petukh* – a cockerel. – *Tr.*

changing the subject. Tired after my train journey, I was not ready for this unusual question but, fortunately, I was saved by the puffing samovar which had come to the boil in the kitchen. He went off to fetch it, came back, set it down on a tray on the table and blew on the coals. Then he poured a handful of tea-leaves into a china teapot, put it on top of the samovar and covered it with a padded tea cosy.

"I have to do all the household chores myself as my wife works at the farm dairy," said Petukhov.

While we waited for the tea to brew, he took advantage of this and again asked

Alexander Petukhov by his house.

his tricky question. But this time I sensed there was no need to answer as he had asked it merely so as to let his guest know his own ideas on this score and that opportunity he evidently never let slip by. I learnt that he had not been able to attend school for long but that he admired erudition and that was why he enjoyed discussing the wonders of the world and origin of the Universe.

He got quite carried away expounding his theory with obvious relish and closely watching to see how much I was getting out of it. He stared straight at me with his piercing blue eyes, hypnotizing me and making my mind go blank. And when he drew even closer, switched to an excited whisper and started shuffling words such as "asteroids" and "cosmic dust" like a conjurer, I suddenly felt the walls and ceiling were swaying before my eyes and fantastic black shades were moving across them. At first I thought that he had somehow managed to conjure up a firmament in my dazed imagination so as to initiate me more vividly into the secrets of the Universe.

Shaking my head and gazing upwards, I realised why I had been imagining such things for suspended from the ceiling was a large wooden bird which was spinning round and gliding smoothly through the currents of warm air rising from the samovar.

The bird brought me back to reality. I had come here to the northern village of Voloshka, Arkhangelsk Region, to see these wooden birds, which Alexander Petukhov had turned out in flocks. All over his house there were wooden birds suspended from the ceiling and lying on tables and dressers. They were golden-amber with bodies carved from fine-fibred pine, wavy fan-shaped wings made of the most delicate splinters of wood, and graceful little heads crowned with regal crests and luxurious lancet-like tails. Not so long ago birds like these had hung in nearly every home in the North.

...A bird with magic wings was bound to capture the imaginations of primitive people and it occupied quite a unique place in Slavonic and Indo-European mythology. According to the concurrent evidence of the legends preserved by all the peoples of Indo-European origin, wrote A. Afanasiev, the eminent Russian folklore scholar, in the mid-nineteenth century, the bird used to be regarded as a generalized poetic image for the winds, clouds, lightning and sunlight. That is, it was to the elements that the birds' qualities were ascribed, and especially birds whose swift flight and powerful wings astonished man's perceptive mind. Mythological notions borrowed from phenomena of nature were also connected with birds. What's more, fantasy gave birth to mythical birds of its own, personifying thunder and storms.

The eagle and hawk were the most important and favourite off-spring of the God of Thunder. The Ancient Greeks and Romans revered the eagle as the herald of Zeus and lightning-bearer. In *Kalevala* the mythological eagle had a fiery beak. The Indians believed that the sparks of a celestial flame were delivered to the Earth by a golden-winged hawk. According to Ancient Greek legends, the raven was Apollo's messenger and used to bring him fresh spring water, that is, rain from the clouds. According to Russian fables, the raven, the wisest of all birds, was a prophetic bird endowed with the power of speech; it kept gold, silver and precious stones in its nest and gathered life-giving water and golden apples. Nesting in the dark storm-clouds, blocking out the heavenly bodies, this thunder-bearing bird caused torrents of refreshing rain to issue forth from them. According to Herodotus, the Scythians considered the northern countries dangerous for wandering in because they were covered with feathers and in England the common people thought that snow-storms occurred when geese were plucked in the heavens. The Poles believed that an evil spirit transformed into an owl kept watch over treasures. The Normans con-

Alexander Petukhov.

sidered that there were giants (storm-clouds) sitting in the sky in the shape of huge eagles which flapped their wings to produce the winds and storms. Along with the eagle, all the other swift birds of prey, like the kite and hawk, were regarded as symbols of fierce whirlwinds. In Ukrainian songs a cuckoo brings news to a mother of her son's fate, and a maiden sends greetings with a nightingale to her far-off relative and hears news of her sweetheart. In an old Russian legend, news is brought to Dobrinya by a pair of doves. Ravens' cries, sparrows' twittering, crows' crawing, the honks of flying geese and magpies hiding in the eaves were all signs of imminent

Alexander Petukhov. Wooden birds.

bad weather. The screech-owl, eagle-owl, woodpecker and swan all had prophetic powers.

The sky is the dwelling-place of the gods and that's why all its feathered inhabitants, from the sparrow to the fantastic bird Garuda from Indian mythology and the beautiful Russian Firebird, personifying sunlight, celestial fire and dawn, have acquired prophetic significance in people's minds. Nature's elemental forces, too, have always been aligned with birds in myths. The sun itself glides through the clouds in the shape of a white swan. Allusions to the birdlike sun are found in Russian riddles where the sun is described as a bird: "There stands an old oak, and on that oak is a spinning bird; nobody can reach it, neither the king nor queen." People used to pay homage to birds and keep images of them so that they guarded the peace and protected them from misfortune. The last place where this kind of handicraft could be found was the Russian North, a veritable reserve of archaic customs, rituals and folk art. But now the "holy spirits" have gone from there, too, the wooden birds have vanished from houses. Elderly people still remember what they looked like. But how were they made? Fortunately, Alexander Petukhov is an

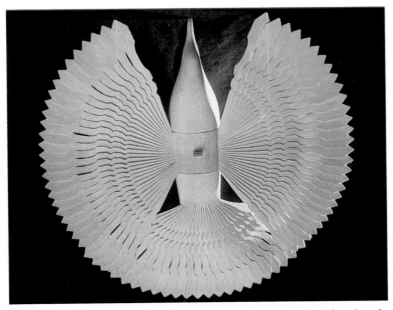

excellent craftsman with a fine feel for wood and a remarkable visual memory. After a gap of many decades a wooden Firebird flew out of his house into the world, giving a new lease of life to the old handicraft.

"In our part of the world they're called splinter birds because their tails and wings are made from splinters of wood," explained Petukhov, reluctantly leaving off his cosmic theories.

"And would you like me to tell you how people first thought up this bird's design and how the first bird was made?" he asked animatedly, hoping to be able to delve deeply into history and again divulge his theories on outer space. "One legend goes like this: since the distant past people in our northern woods have gone in for farming and livestock breeding, wood-carving and making articles from wood and willow shots. When iron axes and knives were invented, it became possible to whittle wood into thin slices and wicker and bast baskets appeared. In those days people lived in wattle huts with walls daubed with clay, inside and out, a lean-to shingled roof, a single window covered with a cow's bladder in winter, and a chimneyless

169

brickwork fireplace. One day a child in a family living in such a taiga hut contracted a serious illness which the local 'doctors' could do nothing about. So he just lay there covered in wild animals' skins – it happened at the end of winter. His father was sitting beside him whittling wood for baskets when the child suddenly asked, 'Will it be summer soon, Dad?' You see, he was fed up of lying in the stuffy hut. 'Yes, son, just a little while more and it'll be summer,' replied his father. And then the idea came to him to make a wooden bird and hang it from the ceiling so that his son would think that the birds had already flown back. 'But I'm going to make it summer for you now,' he said, and made the bird's head, wings and tail just like a real one's and hung it from the ceiling over the fireplace, and all of a sudden the bird stirred and started spinning round and round and flapping its wings in the currents of hot air rising from the fireplace.

"The child's face lit up in a smile and he soon started getting better. His mother came in and for the first time in many days he asked for food. Then the neighbours called by and asked how they had cured the child. Hearing about the bird, they started asking the father to make them one like it. And so, miraculous powers were ascribed to the wooden bird and it became a 'holy spirit', a custodian of children and symbol of family happiness. I heard this legend when I was still a child. In those days they no longer made birds like this anywhere, except perhaps in the remote regions of the Mezen River where the old way of life, customs, traditions and beliefs remained unchanged longer. And, you know, even now these birds are doing people good."

Petukhov was certainly right: his birds really were doing people good, and it was not for nothing that they were held in such esteem by lovers of folk art. And, indeed, only a kind-hearted and sensitive people could give rise to such a beautiful legend.

"Why do I keep making birds now? What do I see in them? Well it's a way of paying tribute to my ancestors and their beliefs and simply because they're things to decorate a house with and make it cosy.

"There're secrets to every craft, of course. The soil around here's sulphury, and from soaking up the mineral salts and sulphur, the trees have tough, coarse wood which is very hard to whittle into thin slices. So, I first boil up my material and then leave it to dry slowly for a year or two and then boil it up again before splintering the bird's tail. When that's done, I make the round body and lay the feathers on one by one. Then I make the wings outspread like the tail, and leave the bird to dry. I fix the wings and tail so that they don't warp when they're dry. You see, the slightest current of air will send a flat-winged bird spinning.

"My birds are slightly different from the old ones," he explained. "They were simpler and coarser."

Petukhov doesn't like imperfect things. He likes even, rounded forms with superbly smooth surfaces. The birds hanging in his house are smooth and have either rounded bodies or arched, elongated, lighter and more elegant frames with crests on their heads. Completely white when first made, as time goes by, they turn the colour of ripe corn and the prominent wood grain seems to add to the feathers on their polished breasts. In a word, they're quite delightful.

"Why did they make them simpler in the old days and not so finished?" I asked the craftsman. On this score Petukhov had his own ideas, too, which like his other secrets, he was not fond of speaking about and if this cropped up in a conversation. he at once fell silent and became engrossed in his work rounding up the conversation, and his guest felt ill at ease because he sensed he was getting in the craftsman's way.

It was obviously a reward for listening so attentively to his theories on astronomy that Petukhov revealed his greatest secret to me the next day.

In the old days people used to think that every house and yard was founded by a brownie and in order to placate it, they had to carve its image in wood, and, what's more, do so with fifty strokes of the knife or axe against the wood, no more or less, in keeping with the number of weeks in a year. It seemed even the best of craftsmen couldn't make it very beautiful, to say nothing of the not so skilled.

"A certain amount of superstition was involved in the making of a bird, too, but I'm free of all that in my work. My birds reflect my thoughts, feelings and ideas on life."

He chose some material for a bird from the log pile in the corner of his workshop, put it on a wide pine block, took an axe down from a beam and cut a corner off with a hard precise blow and with the second blow skilfully trimmed the piece of wood on the other side and produced a flat tail. With the third and fourth blows he made the bird's pointed head. Next came the fifth and sixth blows...

Wait a minute, Alexander! Stop! But it was already a bird. Roughly-hewn and wingless, it was already flying towards us through the mists of time.

The distaff was old and tarnished and its pattern hardly visible and completely worn-out in parts. But you could hardly confuse it with another or fail to recognise it straightaway as being the famous Mezen distaff sung about in an old song which went like this:

> *I have a distaff from a fair,*
> *With very long top,*
> *Patterned with horses and deer,*
> *A distaff brought from the Vashka.*

Although this song could be sung in many northern Russian villages on the Dvina, Onega, Pinega and the far-off Pechora, such a distaff could only be brought there from one place – the village of Palashchelye on the River Mezen, and "Vashka" is Ust-Vashskaya fair which used to be held near the place where the River Vashka converged with the Mezen.

How many of these distaffs had I seen in museums with the same designs of horses and deer and the same long tops and I always felt sad they were lying idle, like obsolete objects, when only a few decades ago it was practically impossible to imagine peasant life without them. But here in Selishche, near Palashchelye, the home of nearly extinct Mezen painting, spinning is still very much a part of daily life. Only these distaffs, what's left of them, were made not less than fifty years ago and they are the last of their kind.

"Ivan will be back from the farm at four," the woman informed me in a sing-song northern accent, "take your coat off and warm yourself up. Where have you come from? All the way from Moscow?" She settled me down by the stove although it was hot inside the house and barefooted children were tumbling about the scrubbed shiny floor. Then she sat down at the brown-painted ledge by the window, tucked the leg of the high distaff under her feet and with her fingers, coarsened by peasant work, deftly pulled a small tuft of sheep's wool from the tow. She made it into a plait with one twist of her thumb and index finger and wound the thin thread onto the spindle. She was going to make socks and warm mittens for her six children.

It had been a cold summer even by local standards, and sleet was now falling and though shrinking and turning black, the snowdrift under the house's northern wall seemed determined not to thaw. When I had flown from Arkhangelsk to Leshukonye, the only way of getting here, during the first hour of the flight there had been no sign of snow over the Pinega taiga. It was only when we were flying over the watershed of the Mezen and Pinega that white patches of snow showed more and more among the trees. It was mid-June...

Selishche is a mere stone's throw away from the regional centre of Leshukonye, about forty kilometres as the crow flies, but there are no direct routes in the north, only the river which twists and turns from one rapid to the next for at least a hundred kilometres before it gets there. And in summer the water level drops and the Mezen taiga is completely cut off from the world for the marshy taiga is totally impassable on foot. In the old days distaffs were taken away from here only in winter on sledges.

I managed to get to Selishche when the river was still full. The motorship's flat bow dipped into the red clay and I stepped down onto the narrow, half-metre strip of slippery shore at the foot of a very high and almost vertical cliff, and climbed up the gully alongside a stream. Several villages in the area were named after these gullies (*shchelye*)—Ushchelye, Beloshchelye, Timoshchelye and Palash-chelye.

I first caught sight of roof tops and then the houses themselves—silent, austere, majestic rather than gloomy, with dark-grey, almost black timber frames, which had stood firm for centuries. Many of them were crowned with carved wooden ornament on the end of their gables.

I spotted Ivan Fatyanov's house at once and not because it somehow stood out on its own among the row of houses in the street or because its loft was covered with dark-green boards. It was a classic example of a Mezen house with one half used as living space and the other as a livestock and poultry area. From some way off I spotted the drawn figures on the board under the attic window and coming closer, saw they were horses and deer, the unique, mysterious characters of Mezen paintings. Red, with very slender black legs spread out in different directions like a huge mosquito's and black wiry antlers and manes. And only Ivan Fatyanov's house had them.

In the mid-sixties when Mezen paintings had long since been considered exclusively museum items, baskets and boxes with pictures of magical red horses started reappearing at folk art exhibitions. Three Mezen craftsmen had revived the old craft: Fedor Fedotov from the hereditary craftsmen of Palashchelye, and a father and son, Stepan and Ivan Fatyanov from Selishche. Actually, only Ivan went in for painting in Selishche. His father made pine bast baskets. Of the three only Ivan was still alive and it was to visit him that I had come to Seli-shche.

Ivan at last arrived. He was a youthful-looking, shy man with a pleasant smile. Painting round birch-bark boxes was not his main occupation: he worked on a dairy farm as well as being a skilled fisherman and hunter, which greatly helped as he had a large family. So, little time was left for his favourite pastime, which he did for pleasure rather than money.

"When I was a little boy, I used to carve spoons and birds", Ivan recalled, "and I've been painting baskets for about twenty years. I used to paint spinning-wheels

with my father and cousin, Fedor Fatyanov, an artist from Arkhangelsk. First, I studied the old pictures on all the houses in Selishche.

"I prepare the wood for baskets in winter as the pines shed their resin in spring. I choose pines in a marshy spot near the grove – they have to be straight, with even thin rings. And when I've felled and chopped it up, I steam it and then whittle the layers into thin slices with an axe or knife. Then I bend the slices into circles, put the ends in clamps and leave them to dry out. And once they're dry, I bind them with bird-cherry twig. Next I make the tops and bottoms out of pine or fir planks. I measure them all carefully, scrape off the bark to make them smooth and start painting in red, and then back in Indian ink. I usually use a fine brush but when it has to be especially fine, I use a wood-cock's feather instead. I let it dry for a day and then cover it with oil. I once tried making paint from clay in the old method but it ran as I was covering it with oil. I first painted the horses on the attic walls in oil paint but the paint cracked and faded. So I covered the planks with zinc white, painted them in Indian ink and coated them with oil. That was two years ago and they're still just as bright."

Fatyanov described to me how a distaff was first painted with the end of a wooden stick and then a feather, using black paint. Then it was coated with oil which gave the pictures a beautiful golden-yellow colour. At the beginning of the century a distaff of this kind might cost from twenty to fifty kopecks. We know this because the artist often wrote the price, the customer's and his own name on the distaff like this: "1900, 25 kops. This distaff was painted by Yegor Aksyonov. I give this distaff to the one I love." This made it possible many years later to identify the most productive and talented Palashchelye craftsmen.

But when and how did Mezen painting start here in Leshukonye? Ivan could not tell me. Later on I went to Palashchelye, the craft's home where the direct descendants, sons, grandsons and great-grandsons (this craft was strictly for men) of the five families of famous craftsmen – the Aksyonovs, Novikovs, Fedotovs, Kuzmins and Shishovs – are still working. And when I asked the old men the same question, they merely shook their heads and said that the craft sprang up long, long ago and on their unbending gnarled fingers counted up the generations of their families who had been famous skilled craftsmen but they could remember only a few generations, that is, going back to the mid-nineteenth century.

Unfortunately, scholars' attempts to discover the early history of Mezen painting have proved just as unsuccessful. The first written mention of Palashchelye as a painting centre appeared in 1904. However, among the many different peasant household objects still used in these regions, such as bast baskets, boxes, trunks, caskets and distaffs, there are, of course, much older objects. It is generally considered that the craft emerged in the mid-nineteenth century.

But is this conclusion really satisfactory? After all, we know distaffs existed before then? And unlike an icon hanging on a wall which is carefully looked after by its owners, a distaff, like any other work tool in constant use, is bound to get worn-out, and it is therefore hard to suppose that it could last for more than a hundred and fifty years. And when a distaff broke, another was bought in its place.

So where, then, should one look for evidence, albeit circumstantial, of the craft existing at an earlier date if nothing material is left to prove it? When Mezen painting is described, emphasis is always put, first and foremost, on its graphic qualities. So what if we were to look for analogies of this art tradition in the ancient manuscripts which, as is commonly known, were written in Mezen although by all accounts it was not an outstanding centre of book-writing like, say, the North Dvina or Pechora.

175

With this question in mind, I set off to Vassilievsky Island in Leningrad and the Institute of Russian Literature of the USSR Academy of Sciences, better known as Pushkin House where there is a collection of over eight thousand 12th to 15th-century manuscripts, including whole peasant libraries from the North.

But what chance had a few stuck-together sheets of paper, left about two hundred years ago in a belfry somewhere in the upper reaches of the Mezen, of surviving until now? However, in reply to my request to see the manuscripts of the Mezen collection, archivist Vladimir Budaragin obligingly opened a tall cupboard where, according to the inventory, one hundred and sixty-one manuscripts were kept.

There was no need for me to look through them all as the illustrated manuscripts, of which there were very few, decorated headpieces and initials were marked down on the list. There were about thirty in all. Carefully leafing through them, I found some of the headpieces were similar in style to the pompous and ornate design found along the White Sea coast, which prolonged the life of Russian baroque in the North for a full hundred years. In others there were miniatures typical of the North Dvina manuscripts. It was quite possible that these books had been brought to Mezen from there or that the copier had moved to Mezen himself but either way they had nothing whatsoever to do with the Palashchelye style of painting.

The pile of manuscripts in front of me was slowly diminishing when all of a sudden I opened another thin book without a binding, and even started: the red swans on the headpiece were so amazingly like the birds on the spinning-wheels. There could be no doubt about it. (I later saw very similar birds on Ivan Fatyanov's bast baskets.) Hardly daring to believe my luck, I asked Budaragin the manuscript's date. Unfortunately, his experienced eye confirmed my apprehension: the book was only nineteenth-century, as the record in the entry book in 1966 when the manuscript was brought to Moscow from Mezen indicated.

I found no more horses, deer or birds but when only five books were left, I came across two which I put aside with just as much excitement. One had pictures of black and red triangles between two parallel lines, a design very similar to the one we see on the distaffs. The book looked definitely older than the one with birds but it was important what the archivist would say.

Mid-nineteenth century said the entry in the journal, and archeographers seldom err in such matters, being just as expert as criminologists at identifying sorts of paper, water marks, paper factories' stamps, handwriting, and bindings' stamping, and at all the other details which all together enable one to establish the age of a manuscript with a high degree of accuracy. The last manuscript, literally the last – number 161 – was decorated with geometrical headpieces and patterns with the same red and black spiral shapes that were scattered over the distaffs. It was dated circa 1820.

So as Mezen book illustrations were to be found in manuscripts as early as the beginning of the nineteenth century, it may be presumed that the painting on wood, which inspired them, most likely existed even earlier, say, at the end of the eighteenth century. Or perhaps it was the book drawings which had inspired the paintings? But this is hardly likely since it is difficult to believe, given the number of wooden objects with Palashchelye paintings on them and their highly regulated patterns consisting of almost identical rows of figures and designs, horses and deer, that not one manuscript with a similar pattern has remained intact. It's much more logical, of course, to suppose that the copiers used separate features of the already

19th-century manuscript. Head-piece with Mezen painting.

familiar paintings on wood.

However, research may be continued in the much larger Pechora collection of manuscripts in Pushkin House. Why Pechora in particular? Because many of the painted Mezen distaffs found their way to Pechora. And if we were to read in some eighteenth-century manuscript that decorated wood was already being brought from Mezen at that time, we might also be able to move back the dates of the Palashchelye craft.

After all, stylistically, this graphic painting is the most archaic of all the known ones in Russian folk art. Also, it is quite unique. It has none of the ordinary elements of the colourful and smart flower and leaf design, very common in northern paintings on the Dvina, Onega and in other regions. Whereas there is a joyful array of colours, reflecting the glorious hues of nature on Borets and Permogorsk distaffs, the Mezen ones have extremely laconic and stark designs. The conventional horses and birds, which look like the work of a small child, are quite unlike the full-blooded, true-to-life designs found on the distaffs from other parts of the Arkhangelsk region.

And yet, despite all this apparent lack of skill and the primitive technique used in the drawing, what amazing harmony and grace, and how precisely conveyed is the rhythm of the animals, flying like the wind, and how superbly the main characteristics of a horse, deer and swan are presented with the simplest of means! It is namely these qualities that strike us on rock drawings, fine examples of which, incidentally, were found quite recently on the shores of Lake Onega and the White Sea. So, perhaps the roots of enigmatic Mezen painting stretch back four thousand years to these petroglyphs or to others yet to be discovered? According to Anatoly Bakushinsky, a leading specialist in peasant art, the paintings on Mezen distaffs reflect a set of very early tillers' notions relating to a primitive tribal way of life.

Certain scholars are inclined to think that the triangles, diamonds, squares and sun signs in the painting's pattern and its graphic elements testify to the fact that it is based on geometrical wood-carvings in which all these elements are found. And, indeed, the horse figures on some of the distaffs from Gorodets on the Volga vaguely resemble the Mezen red horses.

But archaic Palashchelye painting is possibly descended from the ancient art of the Chud, an Ugro-Finnish tribe who once lived in these parts. After all, during the excavations of graves the same rows of horses were found in the patterns decorating the bronze pectorals, dating back to the Azelin culture of the 3rd to 5th centuries! A curious legend is linked to the village of Chuchepala near Palashchelye. The old folks say that long ago a Chud town used to stand on a high hill near the village. One winter day the Novgorodians who had come to settle here (the Novgorodian colonization of the North began at about the beginning of the 12th century) made a surprise attack on the town and chased its inhabitants down to the river. And here in an unfrozen patch of the river almost all the Chud people were supposedly killed. Hence the name Chuchepala and the meadow nearby is still commonly known as Krovavy Plyos (Bloody Reach) or Krovo. However, the Novgorodians certainly did not always treat the local tribes in this manner. On the contrary, they usually kept on good terms with them, trading and exchanging everyday wares which might, of course, have been decorated with marvellous patterns.

Perhaps the most unusual opinion is held by V. Voronov, a researcher of Russian folk art, who writes that the designs of Mezen distaffs retain formal elements of ancient designs and that their pattern may be compared to the Greek design of the so-called Dipylon, a geometric style of wonderful ornamental painting which covered the ceramic vessels found in the Dipylon cemetery in Athens, and related to the 8th century B. C. Today it is hard to say which of the hypotheses is nearer to the truth. We would most likely get closer to finding the answer if we were to succeed in deciphering the meaning of the distaff's design as a whole, and there is hardly any doubt that it did have some significance, if only because the painting always had a strict pattern. The tops of the small streamlined distaff with rounded lower corners to which the tow is attached, are decorated with knobs shaped rather like Northern wooden church steeples, and these knobs have bands of drawings and patterns. Above run the mysterious cuneiform lines or criss-cross netting with commas and spirals all around. Below there are rows of horses and deer, and then lower still, the same geometrical pattern again, enclosed by two wide horizontal red bands with a wavy black line running right across the distaff's surface. And the small horse figures appear again by its narrow "neck" at the very base of the surface. And there are dots and dashes and little stars everywhere, splashed about, as though at random, imitating, as it were, the vortical speed of a gallop. The distaffs also have pictures of swans drawn in one fine stroke. And it was only on the back where the tow was attached that the craftsman was able to give way to his flights of fantasy and paint hunting and fishing scenes, sledge rides and even a paddle-boat sailing down a river!

How is one to set about solving this riddle? Surely, by looking at its most important element – the red horses. To find the sources of this image in art, we shall have to go down under the paleolithic caves' dismal vaults where primitive artists traced the figures of mammoths, bison and other animals in the same red ochre. Is it fortuitous that the horse is the most common of all these figures? Hardly, because since the remote past the peoples of Eurasia regarded the horse as a symbol of the sun and celestial fire, giving people light and warmth, that is, life itself. Most likely, the red horses were submitting to a most ancient unconscious tradition, not even supported by myths, when they appeared on the pagan Slavs' amulets. For the Slavs, too, they were symbols of the sun, and their flight symbolized the movement of the heavenly bodies across the sky. The horse figures were in the sanctuary of Perun. Consequently, the horses' flight on Mezen distaffs might have symbolized the sun's course or the passage of time, just as on early carved distaffs the sun's course across the sky was signified by an arc of solar signs in a circle of crosses or rosettes, a device well-known in the ancient Tripolye culture.

But what do the speeding deer and elks signify? The remote taiga-covered Mezen area once formed the extreme northern border of Slav territory where it drew nearer to the primitive world of hunters and fishermen, a vast expanse of land from the Kola Peninsula to the Pacific Ocean. A major part of its way of life, beliefs and myths was played by the principal objective of the hunt, the source of life, the divine deer Golden Horns. So why should we not suppose that under the rows of fiery horses in this design the deer also fulfilled a role similar to the one on

179

the Huzul painted eggs? Especially, as the pictures of celestial deer and elks were found quite frequently in old Russian embroidery, particularly in the North where they or a woman's figure with horns dominated over the entire composition, and two deer standing at the side of "the tree of life" was a common subject in Europe.

If the ancient cave drawings executed a thousand years earlier reflect the various stages of man's development, then why shouldn't notions relating to different temporal strata have been recorded on the distaff, like in a matrix? After all, the sketchy triangles, squares and dotted diamonds on a Mezen spinning-wheel were linked through archeological findings to the afore-mentioned Tripolye culture of ancient South-Eastern European landtillers and deciphered as symbols of ploughed and cultivated fields.

The two black wavy lines between red bands, similar to those always depicted on carved spinning-wheels, are symbols of water, and, who knows, perhaps they may turn out to be the "two rivers of the Universe" from the myths of the Ugro-Finnish hunting tribes, thus testifying to the cosmogonical character of the distaff's general composition.

But why, then, do the figures of the celestial horses reappear below ground, as it were, at the base of the distaff? Here we are aided by the distaffs which are decorated below in exactly the same manner with solar signs alongside a pangolin, a dweller of the underworld. According to historians, they signify the subterranean nocturnal sun and the whole composition thus conveys its daily cycle, reflecting the geocentric model firmly implanted in people's minds since time immemorial. The scenes from ordinary life, which appeared on 19th-century distaffs, do not really distort this scheme of things in so far as they convey the idea of "earth" by a new means.

So, the pictures on the distaffs convey a day in man's life, comprising many thousands of such days? But what if we were to try and look at its symbols not just from the viewpoint of its design but in a wider sense, from the meaning this work implement had not only in man's working life but in his inner life as well?

Spinning is one of man's oldest crafts. In the Neolithic Age he was already spinning threads to make fishing nets and clothing, and primitive distaffs are found in the archeological excavations of early periods. Long ago spun thread became an allegory for the thread of life and the thread of Destiny. Spinning became a sacred craft and the spinning-wheel itself acquired sacred significance. The expression "the thread of life" exists among nearly all the Indo-European peoples. In ancient mythology the three daughters of Destiny – Tyche – were spinners: Clotho spun the thread of human life, Lachesis, the Disposer of Lots, accompanied man through all the obstacles of life and old Atropos cut off the thread. And as soon as a baby was born, the Fates started spinning the thread of his or her life.

The Slavs have also had notions of the deity of Destiny time out of mind. In Serb mythology, for instance, Srecha, a beautiful maiden spinning golden thread and looking after man's well-being, his cornfields and herds is juxtaposed with Nesrecha, evil destiny, who tries to shrink the thread of life and cut it off. In many tales the Sun's mother appears as a prophetic spinner, spinning gold tow on a gold distaff and giving wandering heroes wise advice. To solve riddles, the young hero of a Czech tale sets off towards the Sun, golden-haired Grandfather Vseved whose spinner mother receives him and comforts him in her lap in the west in the evenings. And in the morning the Sun awakes, takes leave of his mother and flies through her

Ivan Fatyanov. Birch-bark boxes.

eastern window to begin his daily travels.

According to an exceptionally poetic Lithuanian legend, as soon as a baby is born, the spinner Verpeia, sitting solemnly in the skies, starts spinning the thread of life and fastens one end to a new star which always appears when someone is born. And when the someone is about to die, Verpeia cuts the thread, and the star falls and burns out as soon as he dies.

Another version of this tale tells of seven spinners the first of whom, Verpeia, spins the thread of man's life from tow given her by the supreme deity, the second winds the spun thread and makes the base out of it, the third weaves a canvas, the fourth tries to cast spells over the other three with songs and stories, and when they succumb, she spoils their work, thus bringing misfortunes, disputes, sicknesses and other woes to man; the fifth sister counteracts her by not letting her spoil the canvas and urging her sisters to keep working; and when she succeeds, man lives in peace and harmony. The sixth cuts the canvas and the person dies. Finally, the seventh sister washes the finished canvas and entrusts it to the supreme deity. Out of this cloth is woven the burial shroud which the deceased must wear when cross-

ing into the next world so as to always keep the history of his life, joys and sorrows in front of him.

The history of all life... The eternal rivers of the Universe, the sky overhead and the dazzling fiery horse galloping across the sky every day and then hiding underground at night; herds of deer, which gave man food and clothing, and the golden cornfields which replaced them, and many centuries later, the steamer on the river, that is, the whole history of man's life, his birth, struggle for existence, daily life, work, hopes, dreams. And in this wonderful chronicle of humanity each new generation of children of the Universe adds a line of its own.

...The evening before Ivan Fatyanov had brought out a bast basket, plucked a

Ivan Fatyanov.

feather from a woodcock's tail, prepared the black Indian ink and red gouache, and in the morning when the huge dazzlingly bright sun began rising over the bluish Mezen forests, he confidently painted it onto the basket's lid and there, too, appeared a fiery horse, flickering like the tongue of a flame over this primitive fire. Ivan paused to think for a moment, his genial face tensing as if trying to remember something very important, and he started energetically drawing other red horses on the lid. Fascinated, I watched him working, anxious to see how life today would be charted in the enigmatic Mezen painting by its last artist.

The three-leafed metal icon was so small that the craftsman picked it up from the table with a pair of surgical tweezers and carefully laid it on a tiny tray and then turned the gas burner on and held a burning match to it. A finger-thick blue ray, with an orange tongue at the tip came hissing out of the rubber tube and striking the shiny anvil, spread out, growing lighter, and engulfed the gleaming silver article. The craftsman reduced the flame slightly, and it smoothed out and became quieter and less dense and you could now see the icon through it. Fire is an essential element in the ancient art of enamel-making. For many a century it has served people and people have served it...

"The Grand Prince Andrei Suzhdalsky ... built a church ... and decorated it with precious icons ... gold and enamel and all manner of fine decoration," reads an entry of the Ipatievskaya Chronicle of 1175, one of the first known written records of the most ancient Russian decorative art of fine enamel. And during archeological excavations in the remains of some jewellery workshops in Kiev even eleventh-century cloisonné was found. The Russian word for enamel *finift* is derived from the Greek word *finipt* meaning "a light shiny stone". To a Russian ear, it has a certain softness and lightness while retaining the mysterious and incomprehensible quality of a foreign sound combination.

Until the 15th century the Mongol invasion caused the art of enamel, tiles and many other forms of folk art to sink into oblivion for many years. Much later, in the 17th century, the illustrious crafts began flourishing in the northern towns of Solvychegodsk and Veliky Ustyug where cloisonné was used to decorate church inventory, caskets, goblets, bowls and dishes. Even later, in the 18th century, exquisite miniature portraits were made of resplendent shiny enamel. Light Siberian polecat brushes enabled artists to reproduce the subtlest tints and chiaroscuro. A special class in enamel was even introduced at the Academy of Fine Arts and among others, the great Russian scholar, Mikhail Lomonosov, tried his hand at enamel-making.

And a little later in the 18th century, the main centre of enamel painting was transferred from the capital to the old city of Rostov the Great. Indeed, it was only to be expected that the revived ancient decorative art form, which had come from the Russian North, should find a haven in this venerable place renowned for its love of patterns and decoration in architecture, its paintings and applied arts. And from here comes the first documentary record of enamel.

185

In 1788 Rostov masters joined together in their workshops to form the Enamel Guild. Fine miniatures by the best master of the time, Alexei Vsesvyatsky, are on display in the Rostov Fine Arts Museum. The Enamel Guild mostly made small icons, sacred images, decorative insets for the frames of New Testament, liturgical inventory, chalices, crosses, mitres and also secular articles for the gentry, such as decorations, cigarette cases and pendants. The bright decorative pictorial insets on the frames' gold or silver backgrounds and the haloes on icons were very sumptuous.

Medallion with saint from the binding of a New Testament.
Late 18th century. Enamel.

White enamel was usually painted over in crimson, reddish-lilac or brown. The multi-coloured miniatures, which needed firing many times, were considered more valuable, though, in general, still much cheaper than the precious stones used previously to embellish church inventory. Thousands of miniatures were bought by the pilgrims coming to Rostov's many churches and monasteries, and the local masters' works were sold in the Trinity Monastery of St. Sergius near Moscow and in Kiev, Nizhni Novgorod, Voronezh and other towns. When the craft was at its

Rostov Kremlin.

zenith, as many as two and a half million articles were produced annually.

In the mid-nineteenth century first townspeople and then peasants started purchasing the durable Rostov enamel wares which did not tarnish. Powder boxes, looking-glasses, brooches, earrings and other secular items were particularly in demand then. However, quite a few high-quality works of art were also created at this time, mainly, brooches with portraits in the grey or brown tones then in fashion. Vast quantities of enamel pictures of flowers, bouquets and garlands were also produced.

Working with fire.

The art of enamel involves complex techniques, and so it was often a family business. The small plates were fired in kilns heated with birch logs. Each household had various secret methods of its own which were handed down from one generation to the next. In 1877, however, a hereditary master by the name of Konstantin Furtov contravened the deep-rooted tradition of keeping the secrets of the trade by publishing the first handbook of enamel art entitled *Enamel Work* in which he wrote a detailed account of all the main stages of the technical process as well as giving much valuable advice. I saw this handbook, carefully copied word for word

Alexander Alexeyev.

by hand in an exercise book on the table of Alexander Alexeyev, one of the best enamel artists in Rostov today. All the local enamel artists now work at the famous Rostov Enamel Factory.

Alexander Alexeyev, for instance, has worked there for fifteen years. Among the many prizes awarded to the works of this generation of enamel artists, which are kept at the factory's museum, is the Gold Medal of the Brussels World Exhibition of 1958.

Quite a few outstanding artists and jewellers are working at the factory – Nikolai

Kulandin, Alexander Khaunov, Lidia Matakova, Valentina and Ivan Soldatov, Tatyana and Boris Mikhailenko, Yelena Kotova and Vladimir Grudinin.

Each of them has contributed something of his own to the development of enamel art, its techniques, materials and artistic devices and could equally well be the subject of this chapter. In the end, however, I chose Alexander Alexeyev. I did so when I was wandering round the factory's workshops and, on the advice of the chief artist, Anatoly Zaitsev, visited an attic room which had been turned into a veritable laboratory by the factory's "alchemist", Alexander Alexeyev. There I saw

Alexander Alexeyev. Evening. Panel.

a man with a kind, handsome and inspired face, who was totally absorbed in his work. He was inclined over his mortars, phials, scales and homemade instruments, which included, for instance, a special atomizer for spraying on liquid enamel, and then protective layer of glass over the very fine paintings only a few microns thick, which would otherwise be worn off in time. I also saw his unique enamel panel "Summer" in the factory's hall and heard about his long and hard creative quests and realised he was the man to identify contemporary Rostov enamel work with.

Later I made other trips to Rostov and again met and conversed with Alexander Alexeyev in the even smaller workshop at his house. Together we visited the charred ruins of his village, which had burned down during a thunderstorm, and strolled through the nearby roads strewn with golden autumn leaves, picking mushrooms which could only be found that dry autumn on the tussocks of a small marsh at the foot of a hill. Enjoying all the autumnal hues and scents and rustling sounds in the wood, Alexander could not wait to open his sketch book and commit all this beauty to paper as soon as possible. Together we wandered round the Rostov

Alexander Alexeyev. Summer. *Panel.*

Kremlin, under its mighty towers covered with silvery plating and under its churches' white cupolas, sailing with the clouds over Lake Nero. In these surroundings the artist with his open, bearded icon-like face reminded me of an enchanted traveller from the distant past, one of Alexei Vsesvyatsky's pupils, who was so enraptured by all this beauty that he had not noticed that centuries had passed by since. Spellbound by the beauty, too, I listened to his talk about himself, his dreams and work with enamel.

"It's probably not by chance that I'm now working with enamel. Our town's small and ever since we were little boys we enjoyed coming to the Kremlin. It was quite different before the hurricane in 1953. Now it's been splendidly restored but it used not to be whitewashed, and had cracks all over it, and looked very mysterious. I used to enjoy going to the museum which had a fine collection and a lot of enamel, which I particularly liked.

"I often wonder now why I didn't go and work at the factory straightaway, and why I came to enamel by such a long and roundabout way. The reason, I think, lies partly in the fact that museum enamel with its rich colours and exquisite design was

Boris Mikhailenko.
Wife of the Decembrist Volkonsky. *Plate.*

very different in those days from the articles, which the factory put out, such as hand-mirrors with dull designs and rigid graphics.

"In 1962 I enrolled at the carpet-making department of Moscow's Kalinin Arts and Crafts School.

"True, I was very nearly led astray by my longstanding love of music for, you see, I once saw some domras and balalaikas hanging on a loom, and without thinking, picked up a balalaika and started to play. I enjoyed it so much that I soon found a few other students and started up an orchestra of folk instruments. Then I became deeply involved in the theory of music, so much so that I decided to enroll at a music school. However, it was also music that brought me back to art: one day as I was listening to some Liszt preludes, I suddenly felt a strange stirring in my heart, and realised I had to become an artist.

"After studying music for five years, on a visit home, before setting off to my first job, I heard that an experimental department was being opened at the Rostov Enamel Factory, and artists were wanted there. So I soon started work at the factory.

Vladimir Grudinin.
Wondrous Town of Rostov the Great. *Plate.*

That was in 1967.

"As soon as I began working with enamel, I realised that I still had to discover the secrets of this material for myself. Then, too, began my endless experiments to produce a new type of enamel. I carefully studied the material used as a background. "What is enamel? A substance similar to ordinary window glass in that it also contains quartz sand and alkali, but, of course, different as well. Saltpetre, red lead, potash and other components go into enamel and arsenic is used to make it opaque.

In the old days, of course, a craftsman obtained all the components from natural materials by grinding down pebbles and so on. In the 18th and 19th centuries Bohemian potash-lime glass was widely used. It was ground in a stone mortar with water into a greyish pulp which was smeared on the top and bottom of a copper plate and fired on coals in a kiln. After the first firing the copper plate still showed through the layer of glass and so another thick opaque layer of glaze was applied and then a third layer of crushed milky-white glass beads, which gave it a deep milky colour. Then the plate was fired several times with a coating of paint, and this was perhaps the most important part of the process because the temperature had to be high enough for the paint to fuse with the enamel but not to start a chemical reaction with it.

"Nowadays nobody has to gather pebbles because there are plenty of sufficiently pure chemical substances and ready enamels which are made, for instance, for the famous china factory in Dulyovo near Moscow. We used them at our factory too, and it was with them that I first began experimenting. From all the ready-made Dulyovo enamels I chose the best – number sixteen. Dulyovo enamel does, however, have one shortcoming: it's dry and doesn't have depth. I tried to improve it by grinding it in a mortar with a vitreous substance. I realised a material could only become homogeneous after it had been melted, very carefully mixed and then melted again in a crucible.

"After being melted, it acquired quite different qualities. This was true of enamel, too. Its quality improved although it was still far from being as good as old enamel.

"So I recorded the test plates and experiments in an album. In this one," Alexander showed me a test plate marked down as number eleven in the album, "something started happening. I gave it to my artist friend, Nikolai Kulandin and he drew a landscape on it which he was quite pleased with. And this enamel, number thirty, is interesting. I started intuitively using cut-glass and other components and the enamel turned out quite well, at least, better than the very best Dulyovo enamel. My first work in this sort of enamel was a panel entitled "Vsesvyatsky's Workshop" of Rostov enamel-workers of the 18th century. The enamel's deep and beautiful, like mother-of-pearl, opalescent, tough and suitable for all colours. I obtained it quite by chance as a result of combining various substances at random and thanks to my absent-mindedness: I left it to heat up in a kiln and only remembered about it when the material had already fused slightly.

"But even so the time came when I started making enamel from natural and not ready-made materials. I collect pebbles in my native village of Osoyevo and at the Dibolovsky Rapids on River Sara. I calcinate them in a muffle kiln at eight hundred degrees Celsius, and then toss them in water and they instantly crumble. In a mortar I then grind pure quartz to the consistency of flour and add red lead, potash, borax, saltpetre, soda, calcium oxide and arsenic, just like in the old days, and melt them all down by my own method.

194

"The Dulyovo paints we use at our factory are really intended for china on which they are fired for several hours. They melt on the surface, change, and become transparent but it only takes ten minutes for them to stick to enamel, which is not enough for the quality of painting. Unlike china which has nothing in its composition that would affect paints, enamel contains many aggressive substances which prevent you from firing it for longer. And so the picture comes out flat and lustreless.

"Ceramic paint consists of easily-fused glass containing flux and metal oxides, and cobalt, for instance, gives it a deep-blue colour, copper oxide in various conditions produces a delicate blue and green, and copper protoxide produces red, colloidal gold – purple, chrome oxide – green and yellow, and from ferrous oxide you can get a whole range of colours from light-yellow to reddish-brown. However, these natural paints aren't very stable and can't stand high temperatures and so easily-fused enamels had to be made for them. Now, however, though there are a lot of new colours, which are more stable like, for instance, the ones made from cadmium, ranging from yellow to orange and even a bright-red which we call 'bull's blood'. And we get the most glorious golden-ruby colour from selenic cadmium.

"This paint used to be made from the cinders of burnt metal, which were gathered up, carefully ground and added to the enamel. There were no chemically pure components – take cobalt, for instance, it had a few insignificant additives, and the colours weren't as bright as they are nowadays but, to make up for it, the old artists knew how to get the most out of these natural, slightly faded colours and harmonized them beautifully. If one were to try and do the same with our colours, one would produce a sharp, harsh effect. My friend and colleague, Nikolai Kulandin, once decided to paint some girls in old sarafans picking cornflowers. The flowers painted with modern paints came out bright and clear but they irritated the eyes and stood out of the picture too much. But the more subdued paint with a blackish tinge made from an old recipe produced a very good result.

"We could, of course, dull the paints. But, you see, artists today come to enamel work from easel painting where there is an entirely different approach to colour and where paints are always mixed in the most complex combinations and never used unadulterated. In enamel work the size of the picture brings other laws into force, and the smaller it is, the more contrasting and richer the colours have to be. If a miniature is to create a pleasing effect, the greatest effect must be obtained from the colour. This was easier and more natural for old artists in the past who came to enamel from icon painting with its pure colours, and could therefore apply them to the enamel. So far none of us except Alexander Khaunov and Nikolai Kulandin has ventured to use pure colours. Instead, we tend to use greyish ash hues and subtle pastel shades which mute the enamel's beautiful harmonious force.

"In a word, in my quests I've come up against both a psychological barrier and a strictly technological one to do with the substances' chemical purity. I could, of course, mix the factory-made Dulyovo paints to suit our needs but I've always been fond of doing everything myself, unaided, from start to finish. While I was looking through our museum's wonderful collection of old enamels, several thousand items in all, I found a number of unfinished works in which you could clearly trace the old artists' methods, especially in producing the right colours. They had only five or six basic colours – the rest they obtained by painting over the colours. On one of the plates I found in the museum, for instance, you could see how a deep green had been obtained by mixing yellow and blue. And, of course, I now wanted to recreate the old artists' colours.

"To start off with, I tried making purple paint. I put a couple of gold leaves in a crystal glass and ground them with a glass pestle all day until they turned into a blackish violet powder, and the finest particles of colloidal gold could not be seen even through a microscope. Separately on glass, I ground two grams of transparent colourless enamel with water to the finest powder with a glass stopper which I then gathered with a spatula and ground again in the crystal glass along with the gold powder. The mixture gradually began to acquire a violet tint. The longer you grind it, the better. So I went on grinding for three days. The mixture grew darker and darker and then finally stopped changing colour. However, through the microscope you could still separate gold particles. Then I poured part of the powder onto a bit of mica on a spatula and put them in the kiln. The powder began to cake and bubble, and then shrank and subsided slightly, and when it had been heated through, and blent with the interior of the kiln, it was time to take it out. The result was a light porous substance weighing two grams, just as before. After dusting off the mica scales, I again ground it on glass until it became a beautiful purple with a warm brownish glow. And after being fired, it became a wonderful violet. So, you see, it takes a week of hard work to produce two grams of paint! And getting other colours wasn't easier. To make up for it, I now make all the pigments and enamels myself. I want to learn to make thirty or forty different colours and then I'll be able to paint them unmixed, like artists did in the old days.

"During my experiments I studied the techniques of the famous Limoges artists who painted their enamels with several coats of coloured enamels instead of paints. It was a very complex process and the artists not only painted but made the enamels themselves too. In fact, they did absolutely everything themselves. Painting with enamels, you come up with a lot of new and interesting results, and by coating one colour over another, you can enrich your colour range and obtain the most varied combinations. I already have several compositions which I painted by this method.

"I've been working with enamel for sixteen years and the more deeply you understand it, the more powerfully it attracts you with its tremendous artistic potential. I have also mastered the intricate art of filigree and other old techniques used in jewellery. And my head's full of new ideas and subjects on past and present themes and from the realm of childhood. I would like to paint portraits of contemporaries in natural settings. And architecture and primarily, of course, that of Rostov is a special subject with its heavenly snow-white Kremlin, churches, belfries and landscape all around."

...Listening to Alexander, I gradually understood why he chose to work with enamel.

A Horn
Playing...

I was awoken by the sounds of a horn playing a simple old Russian pastoral melody somewhere outside where a new day was already beginning. Here in the village the day began with the cattle being driven out to graze, and a cockerel was now notifying all and sundry that this time had come.

I had already met the herdsman, Vladimir Rudienkov, the evening before when he dropped by after driving the herd home. He had taken his horn from his belt and played with my host. There had been a heavy rainstorm during the day and the track had got very muddy and so as not to dirty the floor, the herdsman carefully wiped his feet in the porch and went through into the dark passageway. And then my host, Vassily Shilienkov, silently took an identical bell-shaped horn out of a basket, affectionately stroked its polished surface, fitted it comfortably to his lips, slightly to the left corner of his mouth, tensed his lips and the passageway was filled with the unusually powerful sound of a horn. His companion listened for a moment, catching onto the tune and then picked it up, complementing rather than copying the first horn's sounds. A famous Russian folk tune rang out.

> *In a small little room a light is burning,*
> *A young spinner by the window is sitting.*
> *Spinner, o my spinner, lost in reveries,*
> *With a light-brown plait tumbling down her back.*

Finding the passageway cramped, the song tried to surge outside but striking a thick sheet of rain, retreated to the cosy warmth of the house in a stream of lilting sounds.

When they had finished, Rudienkov and my host licked their parched lips and started another famous folk tune: "Oh you, garden, you garden of mine". Then they played "Over the Wild Steppes Beyond Baikal" and "I Planted My Garden Myself" and ended with their favourite "Little Canary". Then we sat for a while longer, chatting about this and that, and agreed to meet the herdsman on the hillside the next morning when he drove the herd nearer the village. There he and my host would play to their hearts' content without hindrance.

"And it sounds quite different in an open field, you know," the herdsman told me before he set off home to a neighbouring village. And so the next day began as always with the sound of a horn. The night was over and a long day stretched ahead. Vassily Shilienkov set off into the yard to fix a scythe a neighbour had brought over the evening before and I went after him.

When the job was done, Shilienkov went out into the orchard, swung the scythe through the air a few times to test it and then cut a damp patch of nettles by a raspberry bush into a neat heap. By this time the neighbour was already waiting for her scythe by the gates. "It's a good thing I've fixed it so early because now she'll be able to mow while the dew's still on the ground. I can never say 'no' when I'm asked a favour," said Vassily in an apologetic tone, knowing that it was not everyday peasant chores that had brought me all this way to see him but his rare art, that of Vladimir horn-players which had been almost irretrievably lost.

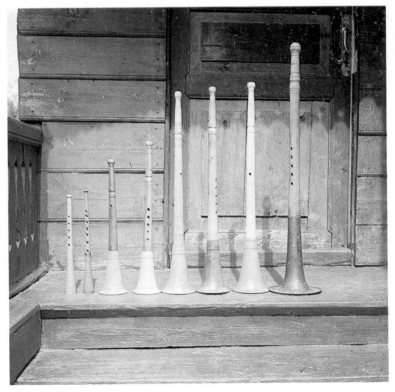

Horns by Vassily Shilienkov.

This art had thrived in Russia for many centuries. Every village in the Vladimir Region had once had its own skilled horn-players who could produce hauntingly beautiful and gentle sounds from this simple folk instrument. In the last century a certain Nikolai Kondratiev formed a troupe of horn-players from villages along the River Klyazma whose fame quickly spread from fair to fair all the way from Moscow to St. Petersburg. Maxim Gorky's recollections on meeting the Kondratiev troupe at the All-Russia Industrial and Arts Exhibition in Nizhni Novgorod in 1896 are of interest:

Vassily Shilienkov.

"'Do you know songs well?' I asked.

"'Of course we do! Why, they belong to us, peasants!' exclaimed the lead horn-player.

"'We know at least two hundred of them,' declared his companion. 'Only, you see, as we play them by memory and not by sheet music, we often forget them. But if we knew how to read music scores, we'd be able to play any music.'

"The men in long yellow caftans and tall fine felt hats gathered on the stage. And then a mournful, lilting, sadly sighing Russian ballad came issuing forth. It seemed as if a choir of tenors were singing one and the same tune without words, somewhere far off. The sounds cried, sighed and groaned..." *

The village of Prechistaya Gora near Yuriev-Polsky was once renowned for its skilled horn-makers – Dmitry Shakhov, Zakhar Shilienkov and his son Ivan and Sergei Yevseyev. However, after their deaths the art of horn-making was not entirely lost and horns could still be heard playing. If well looked after, this instrument, which is made from a tough wood such as apple, pear, maple and elm, lasts a long time. Here and there in the Vladimir region you could still hear a shepherd playing his horn and once in a while a horn-player would perform in a regional club but this became more and more of a rarity.

No matter how many skilled craftsmen tried to make horns, they never got anywhere. Or to be more precise, they made the horns but could not get anywhere near the same sounds from them as in the past.

In fertile soil a good seed will take, even after several decades. And such a seed was sown by the old skilled horn-makers in the '20s when Vassily Shilienkov was working as a herdsboy. He used to tend the livestock and play his horn during the day, and help Grandad Zakhar carve horns in his workshop and learn the secrets of the craft in the evenings. It was then he began to dream of making more beautiful horns than his Grandad's and more melodious ones than Ivan Shilienkov's. But then war broke out and Vassily Shilienkov fought in the Volkhov marshes. When it was over, he helped get the devastated country's farming going again, along with everyone else, and had no time for making horns. On a collective farm there is always plenty of work for a skilled pair of hands, and he worked as a painter, carpenter, cabinet-maker, tinsmith and cartwright.

But there is a time for everything, and the time came to remember that the Vladimir region was famous not only for its tractors and printed cotton; the time came for the seed, which had been sown in Prechistaya Gora forty years earlier, to sprout. Nearing retirement age, Vassily still cherished his lifetime dream and there was still strength in his hands, which were now skilled at so many different crafts.

And so in the mid-sixties he began making horns from memory. He made alterations to his joiner's bench. Shilienkov surpassed his teachers in ingenuity. With his

---

* M. Gorky. "Brief Notes", *Nizhegorodsky listok*, July 10, 1896.

Shepherd's song.

own hands he made no less than fifty different special tools for all the various stages of work.

Then he hung them all on the wall by his joiner's bench and kept a separate box full of ingenious curved chisels and knives for the final stages of the work on the horn. An unusually strong shaft of light, quite adequate for working in, comes from the small window directly opposite the bench and in the evening he hangs a portable powerful lamp on the wall. His daily life is organised around his favourite pastime for he has no illusions as to the amount of time allotted to him by destiny and cherishes every moment. In my honour a hot breakfast was served but if it had not been for me, Shilienkov would hardly have wasted so much time.

And now we were by his bench and he was getting his material out of a basket – a bar of light-coloured wood, rectangular at one end and cylindrical at the other.

"I saw logs of the right sort of wood into blocks, the length of a horn and then chop the block in four, right across the centre," Shilienkov explained, "and then I grind down the log's butt ends by putting the rectangular end in the centre of the handwheel and the round end in a special holder."

With his left hand Shilienkov took down from the wall a very fine bit – a metal rod, twice as thin as a pencil, sharpened in a special manner and mounted to a polished wooden handle, and with his right, he pulled down the handwheel's driving belt. The connecting rod passed through the middle and the craftsman pressed his foot down hard on the pedals. I instantly recalled my grandmother sewing on her old Singer treadle sewing-machine in the evenings.

As the block of wood span round quickly, the craftsman guided the chisel at right angles into its butt end, and the drill slowly penetrated the wood. After wiping off the tiny sawdust shavings, Shilienkov did the same again and when the bit had penetrated several centimetres, he took a slightly thicker bit down from the wall and set it in motion.

Now it was my turn to press on the pedal because he was totally occupied by chiselling. My foot tired quickly – it was as strenuous as pedalling up a steep hill. I changed feet but soon tired again. However, I forced myself to keep going by reminding myself that this small gaunt craftsman, going on sixty-seven, pedalled away for hours at a time. You see, each block had to be bored through with no less than five bits, each bigger than the one before. Then the bell mouth was chiselled with several different blades. And this was just an ordinary horn: a bass horn was twice as long, that is, nearly a metre in length! So, it took not only skill but considerable strength to make this seemingly rudimentary folk instrument. And this was possibly why the craftsman, much to his annoyance, could not find apprentices.

After a whole morning of hard work we only managed to chisel one horn, and that was only half the work done. The craftsman put it under the roof where about a dozen similarly chiselled horns were laid out to dry, and said, "The most important part of a horn is, of course, its sound. Each one must have a pure and powerful sound, and no false notes. I've got one finished horn and we'll tune it now."

He went over to a corner of his workshop where the bellows of a small harmonica with a keyboard were fixed to the wall.

"I made this tuning fork myself," said the craftsman, turning the pointer to 'G', pressing on the bellows and blowing into the horn. I could not make out the different keys but he was already a-tinkering with a tiny bit inside the horn. After a third or fourth tuning he put the instrument back, satisfied.

"That's a fine horn I've made. I'll send it to Vladivostok."

"Why so far?"

"Not long ago I got a letter from a blind musician there. He'd heard about the horns and asked me to make him one. You see, my instruments aren't played by shepherds any more: nowadays horns are played in concert halls and not meadows. It's a pity, of course, but at the same time a good thing too. In the old days, too, horn-players were not only shepherds but first-class musicians. There were famous horn-players in the Vladimir region as early as the 18th century and then whole troupes, 'choirs' as they were then called, emerged. The shepherds used to compete at fairs to find out who played best. The shepherds of Prechistaya Gora, for instance, have long since been famed for their talented playing. In the summertime they used to go for earnings to other districts. In the '20s I myself tended livestock on the River Mstera. I had a large herd – seven hundred heads of cattle. And all the seven young lads in the team of shepherds knew lots of songs; and they played beautifully too. Nowadays we may get invited to any town with our music, even abroad, maybe. After all, in the old days, you know, Russian horn-players used to perform in Paris.

"There are some good amateur horn-players about nowadays. Over twenty troupes are now playing on my instruments – the Vladimir Rus Troupe, the Pyatnitsky Orchestra of Folk Instruments, the Gnesins' Moscow Institute Ensemble, to name but a few.

"Such a musical troupe usually consists of a bass, two half-basses, a first horn and an ordinary horn. Only the latter is made of one piece of wood, I chisel the bell mouth for the others separately and then glue it to the stem. Just now I've added another old Russian instrument to this set – its bell mouth is slightly narrower than a horn's and it has a detachable copper stem and a reed with a nut inside. So far I've made two types: one of a whole piece of wood and the other of separate parts. And later on I want to learn to make a pipe."

The hours sped by as we talked and it was now time to go and meet Rudienkov. In keeping with an old shepherds' custom, Vassily Shilienkov tucked his first horn in the belt under his shirt and we set off across the village towards the meadow. It had brightened up since the early morning, the sun had come out and the grass was glistening with dew. The herd was already approaching the village. We met the herdsman by a small pond with a drooping old white willow. Very little was said just like the day before. I sensed that the friends' horn duet was something of a ritual which excluded noise and chatter. Rudienkov took out his horn and walked quickly down towards the pond, scooped up some water with his horn's bell mouth and it came pouring out the other end. The herdsboy led the cows into the village and then the horn's melodious sounds began lilting from the hillside. They played in a serious and intent manner and the sounds soared freely over the clover fields, copses and wafted down towards the River Koloksha's water-meadow, a truly beautiful landscape.

They played for a long time without stopping. Then Rudienkov told me about how his father had taught him to play the horn. He himself had been tending livestock since 1927 and had never been without his horn. When the old horn which had once belonged to his father, was no longer any good he was fortunate enough to meet Shilienkov. And they had been playing together in their free time ever since. Not long ago an amateur musicians' regional contest was held in Yuriev-Polsky and they had intended to play a duet but he had not managed to get away from work. So, Shilienkov had gone on his own and come back with a diploma. Now they were practising for the next contest.

Vassily Shilienkov was very keen on seeing me off but as it was about twelve kilometres straight through the woods to the main road, I refused to let him. After saying goodbye to the musicians, I cut across the meadow and walked along the edge of the field of peas, accompanied by a horn's melodious sounds.

A Rainbow in the Window

After plunging out of the hot Turkestan sands and cooling its rays slightly in the Caspian Sea, the sun alighted on Baku's ancient buildings along the coast. At its zenith in the late morning it shone on the high walls of the Palace of Shirvan Shahs. The enigmatic decorative lettering stood out starkly on the hundreds of stone slabs displayed in the inner courtyard. Deep black shadows were lying in the grooves and the prominent surfaces of the hard, light-coloured Apsheron limestone became so dazzlingly bright in the sunlight that it hurt one's eyes to look at them. Hundreds of pages of this stone book, known as the Bayil Stones, each weighing one hundred kilograms, have been retrieved by archeologists from the bottom of Baku Bay, and scientists are now trying to decipher their meaning.

Instead of lingering by these white stones, tourists hurried on towards the Divan-Khan, Mausoleum of the Dervish and Dzhuma Mechet (the Mosque). A motley crowd flashed past a small, stocky, black-haired man who was standing still by one of the stones. And now he was left all alone, or rather all alone with his silent companions. He always came here when he visited Baku from his native Sheki, and gazed for a long time at the mysterious patterns.

The relief letters, vestiges of the unknown remote past, drew him here and their fine, clear and elegant lines fascinated him and made him want to solve their enigma and read the ancient master's thoughts which were carved on the slabs.

He knew that the *usta*, as consummate masters were reverently called in Azerbaijan, knew how to hide the meaning of their designs from an uninitiated eye. Looking up from the Bayil Stones, one's gaze slid across the intricately patterned stone portal of the Turbe, the burial vault of the Shirvan Shahs.

"The greatest sultan, the great Shirvan Shah ... the protector of religion, Khalil-Ulla I ordered this sacred burial-vault to be built for his mother and son in the year eight hundred and thirty-nine," (1435-1436) read the inscription above the doorway, and the top of the portal bore an inscription from the Koran, glorifying Allah. And the whole surface was covered by a most exquisite intricate stone pattern designed by the superb artist. But who was he? This remained secret for many years and then in 1945 during the building's restoration a mirror was held up to one of the oval shapes on the portal, and the name of its builder and architect, Me'mar Ali, showed through the most elaborate design.

The sun was beating down harder and harder, and even the wind blowing from

206

the Caspian gave no respite but the man remained standing, as though hoping that he, Ashraf Rasulov, from the town of Sheki would suddenly be initiated into the book's secret.

"Salam aleikum, *Usta* Ashraf!" I greeted him. "Why not leave it to someone else to decipher these patterns! Haven't you done enough already? After all, discovering *shebeke* anew wasn't much easier..."

"Aleikum salam!" replied the craftsman. "*Shebeke*, you say? But you see, it was namely this stone book which made me want to put myself to the test. There were

Stone Book. 12th century.

seven of us when we started after Abdull Babayev died in Baku in 1959. He was the last stonemason who knew the secrets of the old craft. Six were left by the wayside and only I was fortunate enough to learn the secrets. And all this time the Bayil Stones seemed to keep reminding me that the Taj Mahal had been built by Azerbaijan slaves and that Azerbaijan carpets used to be valued more highly than Turkmen ones and that nowhere in the world will you find more beautiful *shebeke* than in Azerbaijan. But this isn't the place to speak about *shebeke*. We must go to Sheki for that."

Ashraf Rasulov.

...Four hundred kilometres, a night's bus ride, stretch between Baku and Sheki, a small old town, nestling in the hills of Western Azerbaijan, which has retained much of its old outward appearance and local colour. Two colours seemed predominant in the town: deep-green – the trees and grassy slopes, and dark-red – the patchwork of tiled roofs. The two-storey houses were made of local grey stone and bricks arranged in patterns.

Each household comprising several dwellings and outbuildings and surrounded by a high fence looked like a miniature fortress. Your sense of antiquity intensified as you climbed up a winding cobblestone lane, thirty metres long and only one metre wide, and saw the stone eaves almost touching overhead.

The sweet aroma of tea and the spicy one of *cherek*, freshly baked bread, came wafting out of an open door. An enormous samovar with a complex contraption serving as a pipe was standing by an entrance to a tea-house and on small tables all around were dozens of white china teapots and elegant tulip-shaped glasses, *armuds*, essential items of all Azerbaijan tea-rooms. At the tables clients were slowly sipping amber-coloured tea from saucers and nibbling tiny lumps of sugar. Washed down by the overnight rain and abounding in fresh mountain air, the little lanes radiated a sense of tranquillity.

After climbing the last steep slope up to the fortress gates, I entered the medieval Azerbaijan citadel where Ashraf Rasulov's workshop was located. He greeted me with a broad smile and strong handshake. He was holding some long wooden rods and small steel tools, polished from years of use.

"Don't you deserve a rest on a Saturday?"

"Saturday? Oh no, I stopped counting the days of the week twenty years ago. I simply regard the day as the time when I can work and the night as the time when I can't. And, besides, I've decided to teach my craft to my son, Tofik, and his classmates. And *shebeke* makes me very happy but how can you be totally happy when you're the only one who knows its secrets?"

His pupils were seated at a long wooden table and holding fret-saws, plywood planks and sketches of future designs. The craftsman set them each a task and then took me through to his workshop. A shaft of light from the high window wrenched out of the semi-darkness a low carved door with an iridescent mosaic comprising hundreds of different-coloured fragments of stained glass inserted in its patterned wooden lattice-work.

"See this door? It's from the Sheki Khans' Palace. I restored it quite recently. It took me eight months of hard work. Right up to the very last moment I wasn't sure I'd done it all correctly, and got my estimates right. It doesn't seem a very big door but there are fourteen thousand wooden details on just one square metre of it! And they're all hand-carved with coloured glass in between and it all holds together. And just like in the old days, I didn't use nails or glue. I did not know if I had succeeded in recreating a *shebeke* until I had inserted the last piece of glass. You see, you only have to be one millimetre out and it'll all fall to pieces. And it's got to be made tough if it's to last for long. I've tried many types of wood but only beech and

14–3

plane have proved suitable. Their wood is tough and dense and doesn't crumble like oak when finely carved."

Rasulov studied the craft of *shebeke* for five years before attempting his first work. He looked for a new approach for every new pattern, and there are as many different *shebeke* as there are patterns.

"In the Shahs' Palace alone there are sixteen different types of them. Now I even shudder to think how much patience I had to have for, you see, when you make a *shebeke*, you have to do everything yourself and you're a constructor, carpenter,

Shebeke. *Palace of Sheki Khans. 18th century.*

draftsman, artist and glass-cutter, rolled into one. First you think up a pattern and decide upon its scale and, depending on its setting and style, you select a combination of coloured glass. Then you draw a life-size model, work out everything down to the minutest detail and set to work on the wood. Here the lessons my father gave me in my youth stood me in good stead. I prepare the frame, cut out all the different parts of the construction and look – this box contains semi-circles, *alats*, as thick as your little finger. You need thousands of them and not just single ones but double ones with slots for the glass. I get very agitated while I'm cutting them out

211

but as soon as I start fitting them together, the work goes much more easily and I almost relax.

"I was once asked to teach my craft to the best carpenter of Derbent so that he could restore the *shebeke* in the town's palace. But when he arrived, he took one look at my work, shrugged his shoulders and set off home again. Why, he said, that's one hell of job. No doing! So I had to make the *shebeke* in Derbent myself, and not only there but in Khachmas and Baku for the Nizami Museum of Azerbaijan Literature and the Museum of Azerbaijan Carpets and Applied Crafts, and Conservatory and then for the Leningrad State Museum of Ethnography of the Peoples of the USSR and for the British Museum. And these panels I'm making for Moscow. You'll see them in the Baku Restaurant. There are eighteen of them in all, and each of them takes a month."

Ashraf told me a lot about the art of *shebeke*. As there is no literature on this craft, it is hard to say when or where it emerged. The earliest stone *shebeke* found by archeologists in Azerbaijan were made in the 12th and 13th centuries. Open-work stone and wooden lattices were to be found in both palaces and ordinary medieval dwellings, bath-houses, mosques. They can also be seen in Persian miniatures. The art of *shebeke* reached its zenith in the 18th century when intricately designed wooden lattice-work was used for beautifully coloured stained-glass panels. And just as the Krutitsky Tower in Moscow was the crowning glory of the art of Russian tiles, so the sublime example of *shebeke* was the Palace of Sheki Khans, built in 1784-1804 under Khan Mamed Hassan and decorated by the consummate Shemakha artists *usta* Gambar Karabagi, Ali-Kuli and Kurban Ali.

Ashraf's workshop is only a stone's throw away from the palace and we now entered its inner yard from the street. Through an open window you could see the palace's main courtyard – a summer pavillion, colourful flowerbeds, a large black cannon and a massive thick-trunked plane tree which had been planted when the palace was built. The two-storey palace's façade, reminiscent of a jewel box, was decorated with coloured *ganch* carvings, its doorways, with exquisitely arranged semicircular bits of mirror and all its windows with stained-glass frames. They looked very beautiful even from here in the rose-garden but it was only when I was taken inside by the craftsman that I appreciated the full force of this splendid craft. Although it was a dull day, magical rainbow-coloured light was streaming through the stained-glass panels into the rooms from outside and it seemed to be playing a quiet soothing melody. I recalled what Ashraf had said. "When I'm tired I come and look at the *shebeke* and they soothe and refresh me." I felt as if I had entered the fairytale world of *A Thousand and One Nights* and could hear the twittering of fabulous birds and rustling of silks and someone's lulling whisper. Spellbound by this picture, I heard Rasulov say, "Beautiful, isn't it? After twenty years, I'm still captivated by it as if I were seeing it for the first time. And that's why I've devoted my whole life to it. But you know, I could make even better ones if only I could discover the secrets of old glass. I've worked all the rest out myself – what type of wood's best and how it should be worked over but everything to do with the glass is much more complicated, and glass specialists are needed. I'm now getting coloured glass from a Bryansk factory. If I hadn't seen the old glass that's remained intact here and there in the palace, I wouldn't have dreamed of making better ones but just look for yourself..." he stretched out his palm containing a few small pieces of richly-coloured cobalt glass. "Do me a favour, will you, and take them to a laboratory in Moscow to be analyzed and help me find the secret to making old glass. They made it in the same way in the 18th century only the formula was lost long ago. However, I am certain this last secret of *shebeke* will also be revealed one day. In Azerbaijan many of the old crafts are now being given a new lease of life. The old masters are dying but talented young ones are taking over from them and guiding art into the future.

Tulips Overhead

I first came across Abdurauf Amindzhanov in an old photograph, taken about thirty years ago and hanging in the most prominent place of honour in the Palace of Culture of a Tadzhik collective farm near Leninabad. This palace was famous because it was namely here in the '50s that, through local craftsmen's endeavours, the ancient and colourful craft of painted ceilings, a traditional Tadzhik national art form, was revived. The collective-farm craftsmen built it themselves and when they had already put the roof on, the most venerable one among them went to the collective-farm chairman and said, "We want to decorate the palace's interior in the old traditional manner, and revive this beautiful craft of ours for people to enjoy." There were five men in the photograph, four already well into middle age – an artist by the name of Maksud Soliev, two wood-carvers, Rakhmishekh Radzhabov and Ochil Fayazov, a *ganch* craftsman, Zokir Nodirov and the fifth, a very young man by the name of Abdurauf Amindzhanov, a pupil of Soliev's. Of the five only Abdurauf was still alive, and he has continued his teachers' craft, one of the most venerable professions of all times here, and made it his life's main work.

I was now going to meet this man who had looked so serious and purposeful thirty years ago. He still worked on the same collective farm and would soon be coming back from cotton-picking, which on account of the unusually cold weather had taken three weeks longer that year.

He was a tall, well-built man with pronounced placid features and large work-man's hands. In the shade of the vines sheltering his small square garden from the heat, he talked to me about his life and work. Seven years of working as Maksud Soliev's apprentice in the collective-farm's palace had marked out all the rest of his life. Later on he also greatly benefited from the considerable work he did copying the old patterns of practically all Tadzhikistan's famous pieces of architecture whose murals had remained intact for a coloured album on Tadzhik architectural designs, compiled by architect and Academician Kh. Yuldashev, and published in 1957. For many months Abdurauf had travelled about the republic, visiting places like Ura-Tiube, old Khodzhent, Isfara, Zeravshan and remote northern villages, which had superb examples of this jocund art form.

Archeological excavations at ancient Pendzhikent and other places have established that the history of this art dates back thousands of years, as does that of the region itself where traces have remained of Cyrus the Great and Alexander the Great, the Chinese and Arabs, Mongols and many other invaders, where Sogd and

Baktria, the Kushan kingdoms, came into being and vanished forever, and where, much later, the Great Silk Route passed from China to Europe. For instance, the town of Ura-Tiube in the green foothills of the Turkestan mountain range, dividing the highly fertile Fergana Valley from the barren steppes, is about two and a half thousand years old.

And it was namely here in this town that I saw my first Tadzhik painted ceilings. After a walking through a labyrinth of crooked streets, between dusty baked loess-clay houses stuck together, one after the other, I finally found Number 54, Engels

*Ceiling painting in the Mausoleum
of Mavlono Eshan at Ura-Tiube. 19th century.*

Street, which had been built in the 19th century and had once been owned by a merchant named Masbut. The plain grey wall concealed a cosy little green yard leading to an open verandah (*aivan*) where the traces of a mural could still be seen. Then I walked down a small corridor and into the main reception room (*mekhmonkhona*). One glance at the ceiling left me breathless, so unexpected was this superb and enchanting painting in such an apparently humble dwelling. The carved *ganch* niche (*tokcha*) in the wall for crockery was also decorated with a floral pattern. At

215

first, it seemed that this was all scenery for a production of *Shah-name*, highlighted by medieval Tadzhik miniatures.

The system of decorating a wooden-framed building, elaborated in an active seismic area, had been preserved in all its splendour. The multi-tiered architecture of the decorated ceiling, divided vertically into no less than seven circles, was fabulous, and the play of colours and magic effect of the designs, remarkable. Imitation beams divided the ceiling into thirty triangular, quadrangular and pentagonal ornamental panels (*khona*), some of which in turn had complex geometrical double flut-

*Ceiling painting in the Leninabad Museum
of Local Lore.*

ing. The central ornamental panel was crowned by an octagonal star-like cone. All the surfaces were covered with a twining arabesque ornament (*islimi*), enhanced by vegetable patterns.

Notwithstanding the profusion of detail, the compositional and artistic unity of this decorative masterpiece was beyond doubt; the room, twenty-four metres square, acquired the monumental size of a palace hall. What sublime heights the ancient art of painted ceilings had reached in the 19th century, whose main types of

216

Abdurauf Amindzhanov.

design may be traced back to the times of Avesta, the sacred book of the Zoroastrians!

The colours of the last century, among which dark-red tones predominated, had faded considerably because an open hearth had been built in the middle of this room in the '20s. There was no hearth, however, in the 19th-century mausoleum in Ura-Tiube and the colours of its ceiling had retained all their original clarity and charm. The column in the centre of the room divided the vaulted ceiling into four equal sections, each decorated with paintings.

Gazing up at all these paintings, one can easily appreciate why the young Abdurauf, so susceptible to beauty, became determined not to let the beautiful chain linking us with antiquity be broken or the wonderful echo of bygone civilizations, preserving the magic signs of pre-Muslim cults, die out in the spurs of the Pamir mountains. In the old architectural monuments he saw the sumptuous world of folk art images, abounding in roses, tulips, irises, chrysanthemums, pomegranates, fig-trees, willows and even fishes, birds, lions, monkeys and horses although the Koran was against the depiction of living creatures.

And then Abdurauf Amindzhanov started working independently. With his pupils he decorated theatres, teahouses and homes. And now he showed me the drafts of a painting in a village teahouse. I asked him to tell me about the technical side of the work.

"We always work in a team consisting of carpenters, wood-carvers and *ganch* stonemasons," he explained. "First of all, the carpenters prepare the wooden constructions and different parts of the ceiling and fix them together without nails, adjusting them to the size of the room. Then they take the details apart again and hand them over to the wood-carvers and artists.

"Before the designs are carved the wooden surface is puttied with a mixture of chalk and gum, the dried putty is smoothed with glass paper and a transparent or coloured priming applied. Next comes the most important part of the work which the chief artist never entrusts to his assistants: the scale of the surface design is determined, depending on the size of the room, the incline and where it is positioned among the other elements of the construction, and the outlines of the pattern are drawn.

"This is how it is done: the main motif of the design is copied onto tracing paper, which has been folded several times like a concertina. The artist then perforates the drawn lines with a needle, opens out the sheet of paper and the same pattern appears on all the folds of the paper. This sheet is then put against the prepared surface and a little sack of coal dust is banged against it, if the priming is light, or ground chalk if it is dark. The contour of the design is then drawn with a pencil along the lines of black or white dots left on the surface.

Mural in the Saidkodzhi Urunkhodzhayev Collective Farm's
Palace of Culture, 1950s.

"The background is first painted and then the stems, petals, flowers or geometrical patterns. The final stage is called *sie kalam*, 'black pencil', because a skilled artist then draws dark lines around the design to make it stand out as much as possible.

"The choice of colours is also very important," explained Abdurauf. "For, you see, it's essential to balance the visual impact of all the details and ensure that all the separate parts harmonize. My favourite background colours are ultramarine, emerald green and occasionally white and yellow, and sometimes red for very high ceilings. For the main motif I like using yellows and oranges. The vegetable patterns complementing the design may be any colour. In order to make the ceiling light and airy, the colour scheme is chosen in such a way that the colours gradually get lighter towards the centre.

"Only pure, rich paints are used. Until the beginning of the last century they were natural and then replaced by dry chemical dyes, diluted with a mixture of egg yolk and apricot, or, as it's called here, *uriuk*-tree gum."

...And later on Amindzhanov and I walked around Leninabad together and visited buildings which were more like beautiful flowering gardens, such as the Music Drama Theatre and Pandshambe Teahouse.

The Young Pioneers' Palace's ceilings were covered with a design somewhat similar to the one I had already seen in the halls and galleries of the collective farm's Palace of Culture. It was known as a *girekh*, which in translation meant "knot" and consisted of an endless variety of geometrical patterns. Both large and small rooms may be decorated with this sort of design. It was namely in this style that Abdurauf had decorated the vast halls with six-metre-high ceilings in the museum of local lore. Here, too, he had used a common device characteristic of painted ceilings: the spaces between the beams were filled with half-circular cross-section bars (*vassa*), arranged perpendicularly, each row with its own colour and pattern. The carved wooden columns supporting the vault were also lavishly decorated. Such was the artist's consummate skill that the two types of ornament here, *girekh* and *islimi*, complemented each other perfectly, and blended together to create the effect of a wonderful garden in bloom.

A Joy For Ever

Bibi Khamro

The village of Uba floats like a green islet in a sea of ripe white cotton. It is hard to imagine that the yellow sandhills of the Kara-Kum desert, dividing Bukhara from the ancient town of Khorezm, are only a few kilometres north. Here, on these fertile borders three colours predominate in the autumn landscape: the azure sky, green orchards and white cotton fields. In spring the colour scheme will change, white will vanish and crimson tulips will bloom. All these colours have been gathered together by Khamro Rakhimova, or Bibi (Granny) Khamro as she is called, to paint her clay whistles, known in Uzbek as *uchpulaks*.

When I arrived in the village, which is about twenty kilometres to the north-east of Bukhara, I found Bibi Khamro hard at work. As her small courtyard was flooded with brilliant sunlight, she was moulding her little figures inside her workshop, which was just as hot and sultry as it was outside but at least not so dazzlingly bright.

The eighty-year-old craftswoman's beautiful face was lined with wrinkles and her movements laboured but her kind vivacious eyes, refusing to give in to old age and infirmity scrupulously watched the little figure coming to life in her hands. A bowl of moist brown clay was standing nearby. She pulled a bit off, rolled it into a sausage with bulging ends and pulled out the front legs and head of some kind of animal, unidentifiable for the time being, from one end and its hind legs and tail from the other. Confidently working with moistened fingers, she turned the clumsy-looking object into a pleasant little sheep or goat or, perhaps horse, and made holes for eyes with a wooden stick. Her toys were fairly stereotyped because she did not attempt to make them very life-like. And at first glance it was impossible to identify any of the animals in her motley collection of loess-clay figures. However, if you looked closer, you could tell them apart by characteristic features such as horns, bobtails, and manes. Bibi Khamro came to the rescue and explained which was a sheep (*kochkar*), a horse (*ot*) and elephant (*fil*).

She only moulded animals. Some of the figures had a monkey on top and many were carrying a vessel, rather like a jug, whose significance the old craftswoman could not explain. ("That's how they used to be moulded and so that's how I mould them now.") In this part of the world water, a synonym for life, is linked with many themes and symbols in folk art. In antiquity water-carrying zoomorphic vessels were in daily use in Central Asia. But it is more likely that this vessel was a lamp in which a fire was kindled to strengthen the mascot

Khamro Rakhimova.

figure with the action of sacred flames.

Another vestige of this most ancient set of magic symbols is the whistle which Bibi Khamro's figures always contain. All, that is, except the elephant. According to a legend, the spring rain (*obi rakhmat*), "water of mercy", used to be whistled for. It has been scientifically proved that these whistles existed over a thousand years ago.

Although Bibi Khamro only made a few basic types of toys, none was totally the same. All the horses in her "herd" could easily be told apart: one had a

Khamro Rakhimova. Uchpulaks – *clay whistles.*

chicken perched on its back, another, a special kind of harness, yet another, a dashing rider. Also, they were all of different heights, shapes and colours.

The clay figures grew noticeably lighter when they dried out, the brown shades turning to off-whites. Then she fired them in a kiln, doing it so carefully because, although fairly heavy her articles are also very fragile.

After they had been fired, Bibi Khamro used a horse-hair brush to decorate her figures with paints mixed with eggs whites. On my request, she painted several whistles that day. First she drew a wide red line all along the horse's sides, forming a circumference. Then she painted in the harness with a similar continuous line, coloured the animal's head and dabbed the top of the body all over with red and dark-blue spots, leaving the legs and belly untouched. All the other animals, except the elephant, were painted in the same way. The elephant did not have spots and, compared to the other animals, was decorated less brightly.

Bibi Khamro stopped for a rest and started telling me about herself and her craft. As a young girl she had been taught the art by an old woman named Shamsi. Here, in Uba, where Bibi Khamro had moved after getting married, there had been a pot-

tery centre for many years and nearly all the villagers made toy figures and sold them at market. In 1924 Bibi Khamro received *fatikha*, that is, official recognition as a potter and the right to work independently. Since then she has worked at her favourite craft for over fifty years.

Work was finished for the day. We carried the painted toys out of the shadowy workshop into the sunny yard and, to my amazement, the colours, which had seemed dull inside, imbibed the sunlight and suddenly grew dazzlingly bright. Later on in Moscow I put her toys out on the balcony to see them in all their splendour but, unfortunately, they did not look the same as they had done in their native Bukhara sunlight.

These ritual whistles shaped like animals, birds and dragons, and imitating the howling gales and swishing raindrops, which were used by peasants for magic purposes for over a century after the advent of Islam, have inspired another outstanding Central Asian potter – a Tadzhik by the name of Gafur Khalilov from the ancient town of Ura-Tiube. Just as Bibi Khamro's whistles carry on an old tradition, his amusing clay creations are amazingly similar to those made in the 12th century.

Everything here is measured in hundreds and thousands of years. While hoeing their vegetable gardens, people occasionally come across thousand-year-old pots and in a neighbouring village, a bearded old man with a furrowed swarthy face will be leisurely moulding exactly the same pots as if the centuries have flashed by without noticing him tucked away in his walled yard. Despite many trials and tribulations, Tadzhik culture has flourished for four thousand years and Tadzhik philosophers, poets, architects, sculptors and artists of antiquity derived their inspiration from the same profound source as folk artists do today.

Usto Gafur lives in the small village of Bufoy on the outskirts of Ura-Tiube. It is, in fact, impossible to draw a line between the town and the village as both have the same narrow little lanes, grey houses, which seem sombre against the blazing azure sky, and the same leisurely life spent by the large households in their quiet shady yards cut off from the street by a long house on one side and by a clay wall on the other three.

The range of colours in this small yard is much brighter than outside: green shady vines, bright rugs, the owner's robe and scull-cap, his wife's brightly-coloured striped dress, some of the region's many fruits which always appear on the table as soon as a guest arrives. And these toys of pagan origin add bright splashes of colour to the canvas in *usto* Gafur's yard.

The potter, a small gentle-mannered old man greeted me hospitably with a friendly smile for he was used to being visited by numerous artists, art historians and people of other professions interested in folk art from all over the country. He was quite happy to talk about himself. He was born, he told me, in this district in 1906. At ten he was left an orphan and taken on as an apprentice by a potter called *usto* Khidir. Before the Revolution of 1917 there were twenty-five potteries in Ura-Tiube which supplied the whole district with their wares. For, you see, clay toys, unlike stone or wooden ones, break easily, especially when handled by children.

That's why toys were again being made for the Navruz Festival the following spring. In the '60s Gafur's primitive little horses and birds with human faces were sold in the markets of Ura-Tiube, Leninabad and other towns. Then he began to make more complicated figures of various different animals such as monkeys, donkeys, horses and sheep. However, this certainly did not mean that all these animals were easily recognisable: the mystical spirit of these tiny fabulous creatures had always prevailed over their great life-like qualities.

Gafur doesn't make simple figures any more – he has taught this to his son,

Gafur Khalilov. Clay whistle.

Gadoiboi, an engineer, his daughter-in-law, Muazzam, nephew and grandson. These days he only models fantastic beasts and creatures. And by dint of their archaic shape and plasticity, these enigmatic monsters, born of his boundless imagination, most resemble, it seems, the ancient Ura-Tiube image of a dragon, the spirit of water, which is closely linked to pre-Islamic beliefs.

"The banks of mountain rivers and gloomy mountain ravines, by the sources of roaring torrents, are inhabited by dragons (*azhdakhors*), monsters shaped like large legless snakes with long manes, huge heads and gruesome mouths full of strong

Gafur Khalilov and his grandson, Irgashboi.

sharp fangs," wrote M. Andreyev, an ethnographer and researcher of Central Asian myths, and in this colourful description I could easily picture Khalilov's fantastic monsters, yawning contentedly as they waited to be fired in the tall clay kiln in a corner of the yard. Among all of them, no two were exactly alike but they all had a whistle in their sides, vestiges of the old magic symbols. Picking one out, Khalilov set it on his palm and stroked the dry clay surface affectionately. There was a frog sitting in the dragon's toothy mouth and perched between the sheep's horns on its head, was a creature whose mischievous face resembled a monkey's but

Gafur Khalilov. Clay whistle.

whose head from behind looked more like a camel's.

I, too, very much wanted to hold this fiendish dragon in my hands and so, trying to not harm the creature on its back, I carefully picked it up by the neck but, to my horror, the top part of its body dropped like a lead weight onto my palm and some sort of hairs and fibres were sticking out of the crack in the clay. But Khalilov put me at ease by saying that it did not matter and that he would make an even better one. The hairs turned out to be from a goat which, in keeping with an old recipe, were mixed with the clay to make the toy tougher.

"And two kinds of clay are needed," he explained. "Two parts of ordinary loess are mixed with one part of a special kind of viscous clay. I have taken many of my animals from old books of Tadzhik folk tales. And I've got a demon and a goblin here and sometimes I'll mould the creatures I've seen in my dreams the night before. I often dream of all kinds of dragons," he told me in a confidential tone.

To show me how he made the animals in his menagerie, he removed the damp cloth from the lump of clay he had got ready, pulled off a bit of clay and very quickly moulded it into a figure resembling both a horse and a sheep. Meanwhile

Gafur Khalilov. Dragons.

his sixth-form grandson, Irgashboi, moulded the whistle, and when the old potter stuck it to the animal's body and blew through the hole, it emitted a shrill whistle. And he instantly reminded me of a herdsman, who was grazing the fantastic animals of his dreams in his yard. And then a local legend sprang to mind: "All the dragons and mountain snakes inhabiting the parts of the mountains where no human foot had ever trod were ruled over by the Viper King (*Shah-Moro*) who dwelt in his capital, Viper City." Then storm-clouds suddenly blotted out the sun over Ura-Tiube.

Samarkand's Siabsky Market is bright, colourful and very enticing on a warm October Sunday morning. There are mountains of melons and water-melons, and endless stalls of grapes, figs, persimmons, nuts, tomatoes, spices and pickles. Clicking along, heavily laden mules hardly manage to force their way through the swarms of people in different-coloured robes, silk dresses, shawls and scarves. The stream of people leads me to the Bibi-Khanym Mosque, famous throughout the world of Islam. Stretching along its walls are tobacco stalls where snuff (*nasa*), a dark-green aromatic compound of complex preparation, is sold.

The snuff itself, lying in small mounds on small wooden crates, would probably not have caught my attention had it not been for the snuff-pouches being sold here too. Indeed, it was these pouches, which were being snapped up by tourists as souvenirs, that caused me to linger so long. You see, these exquisite decorative pouches made of pumpkins and called *naskavak* are, in fact, wonderful works of folk art.

The Uzbeks buying snuff had them, too. They would stride sedately up to the trays, sweep open their quilted robes and pull out their pouches from somewhere inside. After tasting the snuff on their tongues, they would hand their pouch over to the vendor who deftly made a cone out of a scrap of newspaper and poured several scoops of the green powder through the narrow funnel and then sealed the pear-shaped pouch with its leather-fringed stopper. The younger buyers' pouches were patterned and the old men's were either dark-red or ebony and shiny from many years' use.

It appeared that Samarkand had long since been renowned as the centre of pumpkin snuff-pouches, a rare folk art which reached its peak in the second half of the last century and continued to flourish until the '20s and '30s. There are several different kinds of pouches of this period on show at Tashkent's Museum of Uzbek Arts: brownish pouches with light yellow patterns carved on their surface (*pust-naksh*), engraved pouches with a concise graphic pattern drawn in black powder on the smooth yellow or red surface of a peeled pumpkin (*chizma-naksh*), and pouches in chased silver casings on delicate chains – costly commissioned items.

Surprisingly, the small, commonplace pumpkin has enabled craftsmen to experiment with an unlimited variety of decorative styles and techniques. The most famous techniques include *kalyami-naksh* in which a brush is used to decorate the pouch with red and green paints, and that of boiling pumpkins in dyes or oil, and of carving designs and making relief patterns by putting the pumpkin in a mould while it is still growing. Craftsmen add to the natural variety of forms, which range from almost perfect spheres to elliptical, conical and cylindrical shapes, by binding a ripening pumpkin with strong thread and giving it all sorts of fantastic shapes.

The pouches may be as small as a pigeon's egg or as large as a fifteen-centimetre-elongated sphere. The designs also differ enormously. It may consist of a series of dots, traditional national patterns which had a magical significance in antiquity or flowers, trees, knives, people, cockerels, pigeons, storks, dogs, camels and even airplanes and other most original things and creatures arranged side by side on the pouch's surface in the most fancy way.

Pumpkins.

The pumpkin's surface is often amazingly beautiful when it is simply polished and left plain. It may be yellow, amber, brown and nearly the same colour as Karelian birch. The most popular pattern today is obtained by incising the surface.

To see a pumpkin pouch being made, I went straight from the market with one of the best hereditary Samarkand pouch-makers, Zainab Salieva, to her home on the outskirts of town. The art of pouch-making has been handed down from one generation to the next in her family, and she was taught by her mother and is now being helped by her own children.

233

Zainab Salieva.

...If I had not known that pumpkins sometimes grow on trees, I would have more likely taken them for pears for in shape and size that is what these lustreless yellow fruits reminded me of most. However, they were, in fact, genuine pumpkins, albeit, an arboreal kind. At the beginning of May Zainab sows pumpkin seeds in her garden, and in the autumn these unusual-looking pumpkins hang in clusters from the thick branches. And they turn into true works of art in the hands of Zainab.

Before setting down to work, she heated up a clay stove in her yard where the pumpkins were going to be fired. Then she picked several greenish pumpkins and

Naskavak *snuff-pouches.*

put the yellow ones to soak in water for several hours to soften their dry skin and started marking out the pattern's outline with approximately one-millimetre incisions with the sharp blade of a knife. Then she scraped out the skin from the surface between the incisions and a bright yellow pattern appeared on the pumpkin's green surface, comprising flourishes, little stars, triangles, spirals and diamonds.

After decorating several pumpkins, she went onto the next stage of the proceedings and made a small opening in the top of the pumpkins and scooped out all the pulp from inside with a thick wire scraper with a curved flat end. After extracting

235

all the seeds and pulp, she put several pumpkins into a bucket lined with sand, its sides perforated with large holes made by thick nails.

By this time the wood in the stove had burned away, and the red embers were giving off heat. She poured a tablespoon of cotton-seed oil into the empty pumpkins, put them back in the bucket and then put the bucket into the stove and kept the door firmly shut until the next day. After a few minutes the oil inside started boiling and gradually seeped into the sides of the pumpkins, turning their skin brown. The carved patterns, however, remained light yellow. After removing the pouches from

Engraved naskavaks.

the oven, Zainab rubbed them over with sand and polished them until they acquired a mellow sheen.

Just like in the old days, the most beautiful and elegant one may then be picked out and a jeweller asked to make a casting for it. Nowadays, however, it is usually made of stainless steel, and not silver. The metal is then sprinkled with semi-precious stones and coloured glass and the finished article is a most exquisite little pouch, a museum piece, in which you would hardly recognise an ordinary garden pumpkin.

In Yarilo Meadow

"...They make a straw doll, clothe it in a red calico dress, put a headdress with flowers on its head and a necklace round its neck. They carry this doll round the village, singing songs, and then strip off its clothes and throw it in the river... They used to erect a special hut in a meadow, decorate it with flowers and wreaths, stand a straw doll in the middle and put food, wine and other delicacies down in front of it. Then the villagers danced in a ring round the hut, some singing songs, others wrestling... After this the feast began and at the end they undressed the scarecrow and hurled it into the lake, laughing."

Thus, nearly one and a half centuries ago in his book *Legends of the Russian People*, an encyclopedia of Old Russian rituals, the eminent Russian historian Ivan Sakharov described the ceremony of bidding farewell to the spring, a ceremony related to the uproarious pagan festivities in honour of the Sun God Yarilo thousands of years ago and lasting until as recently as our own grandparents' day.

But why were the peasants so cruel to the pretty doll? According to another researcher of Russian mythology and folklore, Alexander Afanasiev, the straw doll dressed in woman's clothing in Yarilo Meadow symbolized the cloud nymphs who sent the earth beneficial spring rains for sowing. But there is a time for everything and in summer the crops need plenty of sunshine. And so to get rid of unwanted showers, in many parts of Old Russia it was customary not only to worship the water nymphs but also to bid them farewell or chase them away, and it all ended with the straw doll being either drowned in water or torn apart and the straw being scattered in the wind.

The same ritual straw effigy with the same ill-starred destiny appeared under various names – Kostroma, Maslenitsa, Kostrubonko and at various folk festivities of the agrarian calendar, always bringing us a faint echo of the ancient mysteries linked with the cult of fertility. However, the straw doll's symbolism did not prevent it from being one of village children's favourite toys.

"I remember these toys," said Yekaterina Medyantseva, "why, how couldn't I when all my childhood was spent with them but, you see, it never occurred to me to ask how they were made. That's why I didn't know what to do when I was asked in the Folk Arts and Crafts Club to make a straw doll but then, fortunately, I remembered about the haycocks. When it's tied round the middle with straw, and its ears of corn stick up, a field haycock looks very like a person. We used to tie our spring corn together with belts which we'd weave out of rye straw. So I twisted a bunch of straw together, bent it in half, wrapped tough thread round it a bit higher up and made a head. Then I pulled a few strands of straw away from the body for arms and sent it off to Penza. Then out of the blue I got a letter saying my doll was lovely and would I make more."

What Yekaterina told me about was a long time ago and now her crafts are on display at folk art exhibitions and at the country's largest museums. She is the only craftswoman in Russia who has succeeded in reviving this ancient craft. And, as we have already said, it's more of a custom than a craft for the straw dolls were made to bid farewell to the spring and not to sell.

The straw dolls now being made again in the village of Mikhailovka near Penza are no longer used in rituals or treated as toys. However, by reviving one of its most fascinating traditions, they bring great joy to all admirers of folk art.

Mikhailovka is sixteen kilometres from the nearest railway station, a distance measured in winter by tractor and ski tracks, the only means of transport linking the villagers with the outside world during heavy snowfalls and blizzards. I was lucky: the brilliant sunshine, so rare in December, reflected in the blue snowdrifts and the deep tracks raised my hopes of getting a lift and, sure enough, I soon spotted a powerful new truck ploughing through the thick white snow with its wide wheels. And so I rode all the way to Yekaterina Medyantseva's house in its cabin.

The winter day sped past: it was only just past midday but dusk was already descending on the village. On the porch I turned to face the setting sun and was relieved to see it was setting in a transparent frosty sky and not in a mist, which, as far as I knew, meant that the next day would be just as clear and so I might get a ride back to the station.

As soon as she set eyes on me, Yekaterina Medyantseva rushed off to light her samovar. "You know, I've told everyone to come in summer because it's so wonderfully beautiful and green here and there're vehicles running on the roads. But you've come now, in winter. What if the road gets blocked? You won't be able to poke your nose outside for a week. You've had it if you go out in a blizzard. I'm saying all this not because I mind – you're most welcome but why are you town folks always in such a mad rush? Oh well, never mind, you've come and that's the end to it, and, well, the main thing is it's nice and warm in here. So, warm yourself and have a cup of tea with some honey from my own bees."

This lively and energetic lead singer of the Mikhailovka folk choir, author of many songs and ditties and outstanding Russian craftswoman was just as I had imagined her – petite, gentle-mannered, vivacious, kind and quite unshaken by the adversities and illnesses which had befallen her over seventy years of life. Whether smiling or serious, her face had retained a beauty over which hardships and time have no sway.

Indeed, how else could she be when she had worked so self-effacingly all her life, and lived all alone for many years and composed these heart-rending lines:

Oh, my love has gone away, leaving me nothing,
Nothing but tender words,
Nothing but tender words...

And then soon afterwards she wrote:

We shall mow and thresh the corn in plenty, oh,
And give thanks for our share of happiness with a song of joy.

...There was a television on a small chest in a corner, volumes of world-famous

Yekaterina Medyantseva. Straw dolls.

literature on the book-shelf, a kerosene lamp on the small dinner table in case the wind tore down the wires, a large Russian stove and a bed behind a curtain. Although a guest had not been expected, everything was spotlessly clean and cosy as you would only find in a village cottage when you came in, rubbing your cheeks from a sharp frost. And what could be more pleasant for a conversation than a smoking samovar?

"I've got to get some straw ready for work while we're here drinking tea. I want to make you a doll." She carried a large armful of straw from the storeroom, put it

239

down in a trough on the floor by the stove, poured water into it and laid the straw in it.

"I find preparing the straw the hardest bit. You see, not any kind of straw'll do. Barley straw, for instance, is too hard and brittle. Rye straw's the best – it's softer than any other kind and easiest to work with. But less rye is sown nowadays and I have to make my dolls out of wheat straw. Three or four days before the harvest I'll cut off some straight, even straw at its roots, bring it home and put it out in the sun to dry. In the sunshine it gets a lovely golden sheen. And then I'll store it in the shed until winter because I never make dolls in summer. I haven't time to."

"When I start making a doll," she continued, "I take about fifty or sixty clean

strands of straw, even them out as best as I can and then twist them into a plait. But why am I telling you all this, when you'll see for yourself. Let's watch TV while the straw's soaking..."

She switched on the television and we watched a programme on the Pushkin Fine Arts Museum. In the shadowy cottage the straw was soaking in the trough and biding its time and Yekaterina Medyantseva, a distinguished artist whose works were kept in the Russian Museum, sat glued to the set where famous paintings were being shown, one after the other. She had been to a folklore festival in Moscow with her village choir but had not managed to visit the museum. Looking at Degas's ballet dancers and Picasso's *Girl on a Ball*, she nodded approvingly but

Yekaterina Medyantseva.
Yekaterina Medyantseva. Baba-yaga (Witch).

Leger's ceramics did not impress her.

"Well, now it's time to start work," she said, settling down comfortably by the stove and picking up her tool – a small board with two thick wire prongs (on which straw used to be cut for the livestock), a large pair of scissors, a knife, needle and a ball of hemp thread. Then she took a handful of straw out of the trough, straightened it and had it plaited and bent in half in a trice. Next she vigorously wrapped the thread round it just below the bend and made the head. Then she put it on a board and chopped off the excess straw with a knife. You could now tell the doll was going to be about thirty centimetres tall.

"Now I do everything by eye," she told me, "but how much practice that's taken! For a long time I just couldn't get the arms right – they'd turn out either too thin or stick out too much." She picked up a thin bunch of straw, tied it at the ends and inserted it just below the doll's neck. Then she tucked the arms against the body and tied them with string. "That's just for the time being so that they get used to being there."

"I usually dress the doll in an old-fashioned smock on which there used to be several rows of ribbons but which I've now replaced with little plaits. So now let's make them. I'll need some very fine wisps of straw which I plait in three or four..."

When the thin plait was ready, she made it into a hoop, sewed the ends together and put it on the doll. The hoop fell onto the smock and held fast at the very bottom.

"Now it needs a sash. Which do you prefer – red or green? Red? Alright!" She wound red thread round the doll and tied the end in a bow. Then she put another plait under the sash and decorated the front of the smock with a vertical ribbon. The doll was ready. She put it on the table, snipped all the stray stands of straw with scissors and the doll stood there grandly with her arms akimbo.

"And now let's make a little man. This fellow'll be much harder work because I'll have to make him a hat and little shoes..."

The little man was ready late that evening and she put him and the girl on the cupboard next to a wonderful little straw horse friskily pulling a sledge and driver.

"Goodness knows how many times I've lit the stove with them when they came out with crooked legs and sides but now look how fine her neck and head are! I've only one more dream: in the old days before Easter I remember a straw dove being hung under the icon and I'd really like to make one like it."

...In the night I was awoken by the howling wind and creaking beams: a snowstorm had blown up and you couldn't see anything through the snowy windowpanes. And when dawn broke, I hardly managed to open the front door: the snow was already waist-high and it was still snowing. There was no electricity and so we lit the kerosene lamp.

"See, I should have kept my mouth shut – now you won't be able to leave. Don't even dream of it. Not even a tractor will get through in such weather and anyway who'll go out on a Sunday! So just you stay here. I'll fetch some pork from the cellar and make cabbage soup."

Until then I had had faith in the collective-farm management's promise to deliver me to the station but now I began to have doubts. The thick cabbage soup was ready and the day was well underway when through the howling wind I heard the chugging sound of an engine, which drew closer, faltering once in a while, and then became louder again. Throwing my coat on and going out onto the porch, I saw a bulldozer spinning round like a top in the snowy field opposite and forcing its way towards the house.

"The dolls! Don't forget the dolls!" Yekaterina called out excitedly, taking the straw dolls down from the cupboard and wrapping the little man in newspaper, said, "Go to Moscow – that's where you're being taken to." I tucked them into my bag for safety's sake, said goodbye to her and stepped down from the porch into the deep snow.

Celestial Herds Graze in Kreshnevo

Among all the countless large and small towns and villages dotted about Russia, some so far away that, even if I have heard their names, I could only visit them in my imagination, there are two, which perhaps not quite deservedly – and here literature is to blame for labelling things and then causing these labels to stick for ever – have come to symbolize in Russian people's minds remote outposts of a bygone way of life. They are Poshekhonye and Vesyegonsk.

In actual fact, these small towns on different sides of the Volga's Rybinsk Reservoir are not very far away from the capital and though there is no express train service, you can easily get there in a day. And as far as exterior signs of a bygone way of life are concerned, you will find less there than in other places. Vesyegonsk, for instance, with its concrete and brick houses looks like a fairly new settlement. Even the surrounding villages with their timber-framed wood-carved cottages and hordes of children who spend the holidays there, differ little from villages in the Moscow Region. To make up for it, stretching for many kilometres along the road to this north-eastern corner of the old Tver region are vast mossy forests, abounding in berries and mushrooms, where you will see wood-grouse, lynxes and bears, and beautiful crystal-clear rivers teeming with fish and marshes full of red cranberries in September.

The old village of Kreshnevo about ten kilometres from Vesyegonsk stands on sandy soil and the road there is lined with age-old pines. The cottage windows are high-up so that they do not get blocked by snow during February's heavy snowfalls. There are old carvings on many of the windows and some of the platbands have been renovated with intricate old-style voluted carvings. Beautiful handicrafts are still very much part of the way of life here as you discover the moment you step inside the cottages. Take Anna Sazanova's house, for instance: it is small, clean, tidy, and light and suits its owner very well – a small, nimble, sweet old woman who is not only the oldest among her village friends but also the pertest, most vivacious and fun-loving.

I had come to see her because she was the lead singer of a folk choir whose fame had spread from the Kalinin Region all the way to Moscow for they went in for a very old form of choral singing – singing in unison, a marvellously original and melodious music. I had come to listen to this wonderful singing and look at the old rituals and discovered that the treasures of Kreshnevo folk art were far richer and more diverse than I had imagined. For instance, the inside of Anna Sazanova's cottage like many others, was a miniature museum with the most exquisite tablecloth on the table, bedspreads, intricately patterned edgings, handwoven and embroidered cushion-covers, towels, wonderful homespun rugs and round mats on the floor. Anna herself was in a traditional festive skirt embroidered all over with ancient symbols.

But this was not all: among all the different decorations and knick-knacks in a glass cupboard I suddenly spotted a dish full of the most amusing little moulded figures of various wild animals and on its own nearby, a very odd-looking, slightly cracked ivory-coloured object rather like either a flat biscuit or communion wafer with lots of little squiggles on top, a horned head and green thread in its mouth!

"These are last year's 'little cows' – that's why they're all cracked. We're going to make some new ones for Christmas tomorrow," she told me in a matter-of-fact manner.

"Are these really Christmas 'little cows'? Why, I thought they were only still made somewhere in the Arkhangelsk Region. At any rate, even ethnographers haven't heard of them being made in Central Russia for a very long time."

"I don't know anything about ethnographers but everyone here in Kreshnevo has always made them to make sure our livestock stay in our yards. And when the 'little cows' have been made, the whole family will sit down to supper and nobody will leave the table until the end of the meal. We used to do it to ensure all the cows came home safely and none strayed away. Now we still bake them but we don't go carol-singing from house to house any more."

> The Kolyada *came riding along*
> *In a painted sleigh,*
> *It drove into Vassil's yard.*
> *Vassil! Vassil! Give the* Kolyada *presents!*

The *Kolyada* in this song, which was recorded by the illustrious collector of Russian folk tales, songs and sayings, Alexander Afanasiev, is none other than the sun itself whose winter solstice is celebrated at *Svyatki* (Yule-tide). This rather mysterious polysemantic word "Kolyada" originates from the Roman *calendae*, and, in the historian's opinion, the rituals and customs linked with these festivities date back even further.

According to the Induist legends of the Vedas (1500-500 B. C.), hordes of dismal harmful demons at conflict with the beneficial elemental divinities sending the earth rain and sunshine, steal the rain clouds' celestial herds on hot summer days, causing baneful droughts. They are led by Vala or Vitra who hides the beneficial seed of rain and the gold of the sun's rays in the rain clouds' dark caverns. He is particularly strong in winter when he builds mighty cities of ice and incarcerates the celestial cows (rain clouds) and gold (sun's rays) there. In spring the powerful Indra defeats Vitra and banishes the rain clouds for which he is called "the scatterer of cowherds".

For Slavs, just as for other Arian peoples, Yule-tide, the winter solstice, also signified the forthcoming victory of the supreme celestial deity Svetovit over the forces

Anna Sazanova.

of evil and the celebration of abundant fecundity spread across the earth by him. This time of the year therefore became known as *Svyatki* (Yule-tide), a time of great merrymaking at which all sorts of practical jokes were played, masks worn, and fortunes told. Later on, this basically pagan festival was incorporated by Christianity in its calendar of festivities along with the day of the sun's winter solstice, once linked to the birth of Mitra, the highly esteemed deity of daylight and truth, now to that of Christ. *Svyatki* last from Christmas Day to Epiphany.

Livestock providing food and clothing, Mother Earth, the sky with its sun's rays

Anna Sazanova. Little dough cows.

and the spring rains had much in common for the shepherds and tillers of antiquity and so they were given the same names. Thus, for instance, the Sanskrit word *go* retained in the old Russian word for cow *govyádo* means not only bull and cow but also sky, sun, rays, eye and earth. Just as today we sometimes compare fluffy white clouds to sheep, so the primitive tribe of Aryans transferred common features of their own familiar pastoral daily life to the immortal gods' kingdom, personifying the storm clouds as bulls, cows, sheep, goats and Indra the Thunder-Bearer as the shepherd of the celestial herds which watered the earth with their life-giving seeds

249

and gave milk in the form of rain.

The poets of the Vedas used "returning light-coloured cows" as an image to convey the dawn and daylight. Spring, the morning of the year, also known as Zarya (Dawn) awakened nature from its winter sleep and brought with it rain clouds. It also drove the cows home, symbols of daylight itself, which had been stolen by the demon of the cold winter. As A. Afanasiev wrote, in one riddle day was disguised as a white ox which woke people up. The spring and summer clouds became shiny bulls and cows, and the sun itself a white or brown bull. By the colour of the first cow in the herd coming back to the village people used to predict the weather of the following day: if it were light-coloured or brown, it betokened a fine sunny day and a black one promised bad weather. In Russian folklore the lusty aurochs, a light-coloured strain of bull, symbolizing spring fertility, also became related with the Old Slavonic deity Yarilo. In *Synopsis*, the first historical work on the Slavs in Old Russia, published in 1647, it is said that at the festival of *Kolyada* the common people "remember a certain Satanic Aurochs and other such contrived profane creatures at their lawless gatherings".

During *Svyatki* the old custom of leading a sacred bull from house to house, wishing people health and happiness was widely known; later on, it turned into a ceremony in which mummers dressed up in bull, goat and sheep skins, and sacred animals revered as the life-giving forces of spring thunderstorms. Despite severe persecution and church bans, this ceremony was still very much alive until not so long ago although it had lost its magic meaning and become merely an entertaining festive spectacle.

There are still rudiments of it today. In villages of northern Moldavia and Bukovina I had occasion to see crowds of youths going round the houses at New Year, performing a ceremony known as "little plough" (*plugoshórul*) during which they congratulated people and wished them bumper crops, and acted out ploughing with a bull, playing on a very odd musical instrument known as *bukhái*, a small empty open barrel with the end of a bull's tail pulled through its bottom which emitted a droning sound.

A tsar's charter of 1648 directed against popular superstitions tells of another curious manifestation of Yule-tide rituals in Old Russia: "They abuse God's gift of bread by baking all manner of dough cakes, depicting all kinds of animals, wild beasts and fowl instead." In A. Afanasiev's opinion, it is from this old custom that the names of various bread loaves (*karavai* from *korova*–a cow, *baranki* from *baran*–a sheep), and of the ritual cakes baked to hand out to carol-singers–*korovki* (from *korova*–a cow) and *kozuli* (from *koza*–a goat) originated.

When you read even earlier written accounts, in your mind's eye you can't help seeing vivid pictures of seventeenth-century Russian villagers kneading and baking these ritual cakes (*kozuli*) from dough, devouring whole platefuls of them at the riotous feasts and "roaring like bulls".

Illustrious scholars of Russian history such as Ivan Snegiryov, Pyotr Yefimenko and Vladimir Chicherov have written about the widespread popularity of this custom in Old Russia. For instance, in Shenkursk until 1780 "for the celebration of the Nativity of Christ every household made wheat-dough figures of cows, bulls, sheep and other animals as well as shepherds. These figures were stood on windowsills and tables and sent as gifts to relatives." In the Pinezhsky district of the Arkhangelsk gubernia "for Christmas they made rye-dough *khozuli* (*kozuli*) in the shape of sheep with or without horns, cows, deer with branchy antlers, piglets, ducks and hens". In the Olonets gubernia "on Christmas Eve *kozulki* are baked from white and black dough in the shape of quadrupeds or wild and domestic foul; one of the

kozulki is put out in the passageway over the doors into the yard so that the livestock find their way home in summer and produce more offspring". In Siberia "it was common to bake lambs and little sheep and sometimes shepherds from rye flour and all these were made as treats for children". And these cakes were baked not only in the North but also in the central and southern regions of Russia, mainly as gifts for carol-singers who sang, "Give us a *korovka* with a little buttered head."

There was an interesting custom in Vnukovo, Moscow Region: on the first day of Christmas a large number of small cows, a large one and two large sheep were baked and on Epiphany, after the water had been blessed, they were dipped in holy water and fed to the livestock. Evidently, ethnographer and folklore specialist

251

D. Zelenin was right to consider that the Yule-tide cakes were a magic prototype of the future increase in the herds. "This was an imitation of reality which was supposed to call depicted reality to life," wrote V. Propp, a researcher of Russian agrarian customs of this astounding vestige of primitive magic.

All kinds of cakes were baked for Yegor's Day (known as St. George's Day in Europe) when the cattle were first turned out to graze, evidently so as to preserve and increase their numbers.

On the day of the vernal equinox when it was popularly believed that the larks flew back from hot countries, women villagers baked dough cakes in the shape of these birds, smeared them with honey, gilded their wings and heads with gold leaf and walked around with them, calling to the spring,

> *Bless us, oh mother,*
> *Call in the spring*
> *And bid the winter farewell!*

In Kargopolye twisted patterned dough cakes shaped like grey hens, evidently symbolizing the sun, are still baked for the day of the vernal equinox in sufficient quantities for everyone to eat at least one and take in a little of the sun's fertile strength. But many more are baked as gifts, especially when visits are being made to newly-weds on "Grey Hen's Day", as it is called.

The New Year ritual cakes in the shape of various animals which have come to us from the enigmatic magical past and are known to many Slav and other European peoples, most likely served as prototypes for our New Year tree decorations. So much for the history of Kreshnevo "little cows"!

...The day had passed without hardly lighting up the house inside: greyish-blue twilight gathered and Kreshnevo was once again plunged into pitch darkness, and only the dim lights in the frozen windows faintly punctuated the invisible road. I waded through knee-deep snow all the way to Anna Sazanova's house and found her already bustling about by the table.

First, she rolled the dough into long sausages, cut them into small pieces, picked up one, squeezed it gently between her fingers, stretched it in different directions, shaped it with a knife and before you knew it, she had made a funny little cow, as big as a finger but with four legs, two horns and everything else it ought to have.

"And now we'll open her eyes," said the old woman, dipping the end of a matchstick into a saucer of water, picking up poppyseeds with it from another saucer and dabbing the cow's face with it twice. And now two black eyes gazed up at me from the plate. The next "little cow" had a barrel-shaped body, short legs and a surprised gaping expression. Why, it was a pig! Why hadn't I recognised it at once? Next came other "little cows", and a fat hare with a carrot and a cow's body. So that was it! It was only each animal's individual features such as ears and horns that made the "little cows" different, even so they were all very finely and skilfully done. And the doves on a thin perch, also made of dough, looked a little daintier but when they were put on the plate along with the other "little cows", they started slowly tilting until their beaks were touching the green enamel surface. "I just knew it – the dough's melted. Nadya! Take it out to the passage, will you, and let it chill in the frost," she called to her daughter.

"In the old days, I remember, they used to make special big cakes which took a whole evening to make and so they only made them when they got special orders from young lads who, in exchange, used to bring them a big sweet bar from the fair with a lady on its wrapper, rather like our chocolate bars nowadays..."

"Gran, make me the largest and most beautiful 'little cow' you can and I'll give you more than just chocolate."

"Oh, dearie, it'll take me half a day but, oh well, if you insist!"

The craftswoman picked up a fist-sized ball of dough, pulled off a small bit and started moulding an ordinary little cow with tiny horns.

"But Gran, how can you call that big when it's not even two centimetres high?"

"That's the way it's got to be because it's going to be covered with *molodchiki* and all sorts of other things and so if you make a big one, where will you put them all?"

"But what do you mean by *molodchiki?*"

"Goodness only knows: they are what they are, that's all. The 'little cows' have to be decorated with something and so that's what they're called."

She started rolling thin plaits between her thumb and index finger with tips smaller than matchstick heads. And when she had about fifty, she started sticking them under the little cow's horns. First she stuck them to its head, then to its withers and soon the whole cow was covered with three thick rows of them, their tips forming a large shell around it.

Then she made the next series of decorations – tiny feet with flat tops. "Oh Lord, I've made little hands and I should have made feet but, nevermind, we'll take them off." But not wanting to be taken off, they stretched out and lost their shape. "Oh, what will I do with them now?" grumbled the old woman, trying to put down the tiny hands which had got stuck to her fingers. Once she had managed to, she made numerous squiggly shapes, apparently symbolizing oats, and the field round the little cow, which was grazing contentedly in the luscious grass, grew noticeably larger.

Moulding the hundreds of different shapes and arranging them all in neat and attractive rows really did turn out to be laborious, long work. But, at last, the final row of something or other was put round the little cow which was now mooing in delight at the fabulous abundance of grasses of various kinds, and the old woman fenced in the round field with a twisted plait.

"Pity I've no beads. I ought to make her eyes bigger," the old woman said wistfully and stuck three poppyseeds in each of her eyes instead. Then she picked up her scissors, cut some green and red threads and tiny strips of silver foil from a sweet wrapper which shone like silver rain on a New-Year tree and decorated the field here and there with them and put a bunch of green thread right under the cow's nose.

Anna Sazanova. Large dough cow cake.

Bread provides one of man's essential needs and for a peasant there is nothing more beautiful in nature than a golden field of tall sturdy ears of wheat whose beauty is derived from the earth, the source of life itself. And this amusing and touching little dough cow is, as it were, a primeval link in the chain of beauty with which man has always surrounded his life on earth, a primeval link in the eternal chain binding the great sculptors of Ancient Greece with Leonardo, and the courageous Heralds bringing tidings of beauty.

Request to Readers

Raduga Publishers would be glad to have your opinion of this book, its translation and design and any suggestions you may have for future publications.

Please send all your comments to 17, Zubovsky Boulevard, Moscow, USSR.